I0056984

A I R B N B

Why so many people are earning a seven-figure income without owning property

TABLE OF CONTENTS

INTRODUCTION

Every single day, day in and day out, you put in ten hours at the office, five days per week. Endless phone calls, annoying co-workers, leads that never pan out, the raise that always seems just out of reach. No one in your office seems to be having much fun, either, even if you did get that promotion the bosses are always dangling in front of you. Then, you go home to your one-bedroom apartment, collapse on the couch, and fall asleep with the television on, your phone on your chest. This is the golden age of technology, but the only sign of it is the Facebook feed that is endlessly refreshing itself on your phone as you try to fall into a restless night of sleep. There were so many promises about how the internet would change work culture forever. Instead, your everyday life seems uncomfortable, similar to the life your parents were leading. You live paycheck to paycheck, under the thumb of some anonymous, and undeserving boss. Every "luxury" purchase you make, like a slightly bigger television or the latest iPhone, seems like a huge accomplishment, only to disappoint you immediately after. You can't seem to keep up with you any of your friends. Retirement seems like a distant dream. Even your short annual vacation never seems to arrive, and the few days of freedom vanish in a flash. The weekend passes in the blink of an eye. You were always considered the smartest one in the room, destined for success. So how did this happen? And, most importantly, what can you possibly do to change this situation?

If you picked up this book, that means that you want to find a way out of this all too common scenario. Maybe you are halfway through your career and sick and tired of the daily stress that comes with earning a paycheck. Maybe you are tantalizingly close to retirement but simply cannot bear the thought of sticking it out for another five years – and you know that your pension check will not be enough to live the lifestyle you deserve, even when you do make it to sixty-five years old.

Inside your office building, your daily reality beats a message into your head: this is how things are and how they will always be. You put in your time (your stressful, stressful time!), you take home your paycheck, and that's the end of it. However, if you picked up this book, you probably have the suspicion that outside the daily nine to five grind at the office, there are happy, smiling people, people who are able to determine their own worth, who set their own schedules, who are free to come and go as they please. Maybe you have read about them on a Reddit forum or in a newspaper feature. Maybe you know one of them: a close friend or distant relative or a co-worker of yours who was able to quit. You know these people are not trust-fund babies, born with a silver spoon in their mouth. Nor are they just the ones who got lucky. Quite simply, they are just people who are smart about how they put the new internet economy to work for them. People who know how to take advantage of the technological developments that are now making it possible for any regular person to become a real estate mogul. People who are quitting their nine to five jobs and becoming Airbnb hosts, even without owning property, and earning seven-figure passive income. People like you.

If you are a regular traveler, you may have stayed in an Airbnb, so you know a little bit about what it is all about. However, for those of you who are new to the concept, the short definition is: Airbnb is a web platform that allows people to rent out space within their home or an entire property, controlling every aspect of the process along the way. Airbnb lets you set the price – an individual price for every single day – and the terms of the rental. If you so choose, it can also set the price for you within your allowed window, based on how desirable your list-ing is, how close the rental date is, and how much competition there is in your area. The site also allows you to communicate with your guests, gives your guests automated information about check-in and check-out procedures, protects you in the event of loss or damage, pays any local occupancy taxes for you, and helps you promote your listing to potential guests. After the stay is over, it also allows host and guest to review one another, and it aggregates these reviews so that future guests and hosts can assess the level trustworthiness a member deserves. Finally, it gives you statistics about how many people visited your listing and how many of them chose to book. And it does all this without any listing fee on the part of the host, only for a small booking fee that it collects in part from you as host, and in part from the guest.

Note: Even just reading through this summary of what Airbnb does, you will already have a sense of the fact that this kind of investment does not seem to be "passive," if by passive we mean that you literally do not lift a finger. In fact, until you get a property management company involved, there will be some amount of work to do – so keep in mind that this kind of investment should be thought of as "somewhat passive." However, do not fear: first of all, the amount of work that needs to be done compared to your grueling nine to five job is significantly lighter and, usually more pleasant. Secondly, the features of Airbnb that make the site so popular are precisely the ones that allow hosts to automatize their listing.

This book will walk you through the steps of becoming an Airbnb mogul in your own right. In the course of thirty-six chapters, you will learn the ins and outs of Airbnb hosting so that you will have everything you need to get started on your life-changing journey.

Chapter 1, "Why Airbnb," will consider the two sides of the Airbnb coin: the guest's experience and the host's experience, explaining why both benefit from the authentic, local experience. From the perspective of the host, it provides an easy way to start in the hospitality business – or just to start a business in general.

Chapter 2, "Why Airbnb is Not the Same as Real Estate," helps you take into consideration a number of factors when deciding whether to become a traditional landlord or start an Airbnb. It goes through and lists a number of complex legal issues that often can arise when renting long term. The chapter explains that, if you just want to get your feet wet in the hospitality industry, Airbnb is the better option compared to traditional rentals, because there is no listing fee or commitment.

Chapter 3, "Getting the Cash Flowing," talks about how long it will take before you start making money on Airbnb. Although getting started on Airbnb is simpler than you might think, it does require some upfront investment of time and money. A good estimate of how long it will take you to start earning five figures of income, is about one to two years, depending on how heavily you invest in multiple properties – and how lucky you are.

Chapter 4, "A Brief History of Airbnb," suggests the importance of learning about the industry you are investing in, before taking the plunge. Not only will this prepare to you avoid any unpleasant surprises, but it will also help you know how to make the most of your investment by conveying the company's values to you. In the case of Airbnb, the keyword to focus on is "community." Airbnb was developed to give an authentic, personal, local experience and not simply be a cheap substitute for a hotel room.

Chapter 5, "What You Need to Know Before You Start Making You Money," goes through the main personal and business challenges you will likely have to face when growing your new business. After discussing these issues and why they are important, the chapter ends with some important suggestions about why you should only list your properties only on one platform, why you should stay at other popular Airbnb's before trying to become a host and who makes the most money on Airbnb—and why.

Chapter 6, "So how do you make money without owning a home?"

This chapter will discuss retail arbitrage, which is an easy way to start to earn money on Airbnb without owning your own home. It will explain how to be strategic when approaching your landlord, showing you how to prepare yourself with confidence in your situation. It will discuss the possibilities of what you might offer them and some reassurances to common fears. The chapter will also cover all the possible local regulations, like zoning and permits, that Airbnb recommends you investigate before you start to host.

Chapter 7, "Money, Money, Money," is the chapter that talks about everyone's favorite subject. Yup, you guessed it, money. We will spill the beans right away: there is no magic number of how much it costs to get started on Airbnb. That is the good news because you can make your hosting experience work for you, whatever your budget might be. Just make sure you have a plan and a business mindset to get you started.

Chapter 8, "Renting, owning and Landlord negotiation," will talk all about how to set up Airbnb for a property that you do not own, specifically in terms of how to best negotiate with your landlord and the risks involved. It will dive into the specific negotiation techniques and language you should use to be most likely to get what you want from them. This chapter will also highlight the differences between Airbnb for properties you own compared to those you do not own.

Chapter 9, "Time to dive in" will talk all about how to research the market and will cover using things like What AirDNA is and why this is such a useful tool to use; how to identify competition in your area; and how to price your rental correctly.

Chapter 10, "What can affect your listing" goes over the main components of a successful listing, including your listing details, your Superhost status, and your guest's experience and review.

Chapter 11, "So are you ready to furnish?" talks about some of the main ticket items you will need to get ready to rent your place and considers questions you need to ask yourself as you prepare to invest in furniture.

Chapter 12, "The essential Gadget list," will talk all about the specific gadgets you need to have in your Airbnb and the specific reasons behind them. It will also suggest what *not* to provide.

Chapter 13, "Let's get some Insurance," goes over the Airbnb provided insurance policies and suggests what to do to make sure you are fully covered.

Chapter 14, "How to create a kick-ass listing," discusses the various features of the Airbnb listing, which will help you attract more views and bookings.

Chapter 15, "How to manage multiple listings on Airbnb," discusses taking the next step in your listing experience. There are lots of responsibilities that come from multiple listings, but it also is the way to earn the most from your Airbnb experience. This chapter discusses some things to think about when you want to scale up.

Chapter 16, "A picture tells a thousand words," discusses the fundamentals of good Airbnb photography.

Chapter 17, "The price is right," discusses some basics of pricing and how to make the most of Airbnb resources as well as third-party apps that give you information on comparable properties.

Chapter 18, "Beware the Taxman," points you in the direction of where to find information on Airbnb and tax laws, which vary widely in different countries.

Chapter 19, "Listing in a tourist destination and managing vacation homes," discusses the ups and downs of vacation rentals. In order to prepare you, this chapter will give advice about how to be smart about your vacation rental, so you can assess if it is the right market for you. A property management company is highly recommended in these situations.

Chapter 20, "How to promote your Airbnb listing," will dive into all the different ways you can promote your Airbnb listings, including through email lists and social media, and will discuss why it is important to promote.

Chapter 21, "How to Manage Guests," will help make sure you start things off on the right foot, by explaining a series of messages to send them as they get ready to visit your property. It will also cover some major problem areas and suggest what to do to avoid them, and what to do if they happen anyway.

Chapter 22, "How to Get reviews," will discuss some ways to get your five-star reviews and get your listing going.

Chapter 23, "Automation is king," gives you guidance on what to automate and why.

Chapter 24 "Real estate and Airbnb," is a discussion of where to find information on the best places to invest on Airbnb.

Chapter 25, "Scaling up" teaches you the key steps to going from a single listing to multiple listings, on your way to earning six figures worth of annual income.

Chapter 26 – "Timescales from beginning to end" provides a checklist of everything you need to do to go from having nothing to having an Airbnb empire.

Chapter 27, "Quick secrets to cash in on Airbnb and a couple of advanced secrets," gives you exactly what it sounds like: tips for making the most of your Airbnb.

Chapter 28, "Slow season," is a chapter that will offer you tons of ideas about how to get your Airbnb prepared to continue earning money the slow season since most people are in an area that has one. This chapter will discuss the importance of having a good business model and how that allows for flexibility in pricing. It will suggest relaxing some of your stricter standards, including allowing for instant booking if you do not already. It will also offer advanced strategies that include improving your marketing efforts and leveraging your past guests by offering them and their friends future low season discounts.

Chapter 29 - "What you might not have considered," will focus on things merits/demerits of weekly/monthly discounts, leveraging AirDNA data, as well as accepting children/infants, co-hosting and property management.

Chapter 30 - "Airbnb terms" will focus on general terms people talk about when it comes to Airbnb and what they all mean.

Chapter 31, "Insider secrets," is all about how to maximize views of your listing and, once they book, how to improve your guests' experience with a simple trick. It also covers crucial details like how to become (and stay) a super host and how to use discounts to your advantage.

Chapter 32, "How to stay safe with Airbnb," discusses how to maximize your safety as a host, pointing to two main strategies: using a guest's profile reviews to screen potential guests and adopting security-focused technology to make your property safer.

Chapter 33, "Practical Examples," will discuss how to create the rule book for guests, including questions to ask yourself when planning it out.

Finally, Chapter 34 is the conclusion that summarizes all the main suggestions of the book.

Suggestions for How to read this book:

This book was written with the idea of being read cover to cover, in order to address all the potential issues of how to successfully rent on Airbnb. Ideally, you would read through the entire book and then use the individual chapters as reference guides to return to as you progress on your hosting journey. However, if you are already knowledgeable about the basics, feel free to jump directly to whatever topic is most relevant. (Keep in mind that each chapter also has specific examples, so even if you feel like you know the basics, reading each chapter can be helpful to give you more detailed knowledge.) In any case, each chapter has been written in order to be read on its own. Also, at the end of each chapter you will find a quick summary as well as some practical advice in terms of the next steps to follow, so check there to track your progress as you go through the book.

CHAPTER 1: WHY AIRBNB

Okay, you are likely feeling a little impatient to dive right in, but in order to get started on your journey to seven-figure passive income, you need to know a bit more of the background with the practice of Airbnb, how it has managed to disrupt the hotel industry worldwide, and why it is such a major economic juggernaut. The only way that Airbnb could have reached its current levels of global success is because of the simple but crucial fact that guests and hosts both love it. Guests love Airbnb for a series of emotional, practical, and economic reasons, that makes it better than a traditional hotel experience. Hosts love Airbnb because of how easy it makes it to get started in the business world. In the sections below, we will discuss these points in more detail, in order to give you a full picture of what Airbnb has to offer.

Why Do Guests Like Airbnb?

Hotels are everywhere in the world, and at every price point, from budget motels to extravagant luxury dwellings. So why was Airbnb able to come in and disrupt the hotel market so profoundly? First, although it does seem as though everywhere you look, there is a hotel, due to zoning regulation, hotels are usually clustered around certain areas of a city. San Francisco, the home of Airbnb, is a perfect example of this: while most hotels are clustered in the urban downtown, also known as the financial district, only a few small boutique hotels are positioned in other charming, dynamic neighborhoods, like the Mission District. Because anyone can turn a property into an Airbnb (except in the cases of local regulations, as will be discussed), a guest who wants a true neighborhood experience, will be more likely to get it through Airbnb. Then, beyond the city experience, Airbnb is also amazing for making more areas of the world accessible rural areas. There are Airbnb treehouses in forests and Airbnb school busses where people sleep in farms in a converted vehicle.

This could be for touristic reasons, such as wanting to more "authentically" experience a place. Or it could be for very practical reasons: Airbnb guests are often in town for non-leisure activities. Many come to visit their families but do not want to impose by staying in their house. Others come for job interviews or hospital procedures. For these people, the wide range of choices in terms of location becomes a serious selling point: rather than stay in the designated hotel district; they have better chances of booking a property in easy travel distance from their child's home, their interview location or their doctor's office.

Another major reason why people love Airbnb beyond the great choice of locations is the fact that the individual, private nature of the technology means that it becomes possible to build actual relationships, either with other guests staying at the same property or with the hosts. Sometimes this could be just a brief interaction during check-in, where the host gives the guest some exciting, exclusive tips about what to do in the area. Other times, the guest-host relationship can be more elaborate, including sharing meals or the host serving as a tour guide for the guest. This, of course, all depends on the interests and availability of each guest and host and is something that hosts can make clear upfront in their listing (i.e., whether they are available to spend time with guests and, if so, how much). However, regardless, it is one of the features that makes Airbnb unique and offers a commodity that quite simply could not happen in a large corporate hotel.

Beyond the feel-good aspect of making new friends while traveling, Airbnb's are generally better than hotels because they are simply more livable. Have you ever stayed at a $150 per night chain hotel? Not only are the rooms rectangular shoeboxes, with identical, generic décor, but all they have are one or two beds, a desk, an armchair, a closet, a television, and a console, as well as a minuscule bathroom. If you're lucky, it might have a minifridge (that probably does not actually cool anything down!) and a Keurig coffee maker with stale pods and Styrofoam cups. In the small bathroom, you'll get itty bitty quantities of body wash, shampoo, and lotion.

Compare that to an Airbnb, which is usually a space that was designed to *live* in. You may be renting a studio, sure, but you could probably also find a one or two-bedroom—or more—giving yourself some privacy from your fellow travelers. (Parents of young children love Airbnb because they can put their kids to bed and then have a nice evening, whereas, in a hotel, lights off mean everyone is in the dark.) If you are traveling with a group of friends, a hotel means that everyone goes back to their separate rooms or congregates in a public place, whereas Airbnb means everyone can hang out in the common area.

Airbnb also regularly offers amenities like washer and dryer (no more expensive hotel dry cleaning!), television offerings like Netflix, Hulu, and Amazon prime, and kitchens that are often fully stocked with staples like oils and spices. A thoughtful host will also leave their guest's little treats, like beer and wine and bottled water, or individual packages of breakfast cereal and freshly ground coffee, making it easy for guests to take care of themselves before heading off on their activities. For traveling parents, a child-friendly Airbnb might have a pack and play crib, a highchair, toys, and even be baby proofed. Finally, beyond the practical amenities, Airbnb's are more likely than hotels to have awesome, private luxury offerings, for a fraction of the price: hot tubs and pools, free usage of bikes and boats, or a completely private deck that allows you to take in a priceless view.

All these perks sound amazing, but what really ends up making the difference is that Airbnb guests get a better experience at a lower price, especially when staying for slightly longer amounts of time, such as a week or a month. Although the rules vary from city to city, Airbnb's are generally not required to collect high occupancy taxes, which keeps the rates lower. More to the point, since the start-up costs are low, and the competition is intense, hosts are able and willing to offer their places for a fraction of what hotels charge. The top-notch algorithm calculates the best possible price for hosts so that they can keep occupancy up – and costs down.

Why Do Hosts Like Airbnb?

Airbnb is a two-way street. Without the interest of guests, it would never work, but there needs to be an equal desire on the part of potential hosts to open their homes to these virtual strangers. So why do people do this? Especially average individuals with no prior business experience, who never seemed to have an interest in entrepreneurial activity?

Quite simply, it is a reliable, steady source of passive income that can make it possible for individuals to reduce their traditional job commitments or, even better, quit them entirely. According to a recent statistic, the average host earns $20,000 per year with Airbnb. Beyond the economic benefit, the Airbnb hosting experience offers much to the potential host, including the opportunity to meet people from around the world. However, beyond this more subjective component, Airbnb gives a concrete opportunity to test out the hospitality market, to get your feet wet without plunking down hundreds of thousands of dollars in cash and committing hundreds of hours of time. For people who are contemplating going into hospitality full time, Airbnb is a great start. Moreover, Airbnb is one of the easiest side business to get off the ground, so it also provides a great training ground for someone who wants to go into personal entrepreneurship in general, allowing them to learn the ins and outs of being a small business owner with little start-up cost. Along these lines, starting an Airbnb is amazing for personal development. It forces hosts to interact with all kinds of people from all over the world while keeping the bulk of the responsibility in Silicon Valley. It demands hosts to become problem solvers, to engage in personal branding activities, to think about interior design, and to improve their people skills.

The growth potential for Airbnb hosts is unlimited. It also is quite flexible in terms of what is required. Depending on your available time, your budget, your interests, and your skill set, you can outsource many of these elements to professional individuals or management companies—so do not be intimidated if any of the above elements (like the interior design!) sounds too onerous. These will be addressed one by one, along with possibilities for outsourcing them to others.

Chapter Summary

In this chapter, we discussed the two sides of the Airbnb coin: the guest's experience and the host's experience. On the one hand, the guest loves Airbnb because it gives a more realistic, authentic experience of the city they are visiting. It allows them to explore a new neighborhood and, sometimes, meet local people. Everything about it is unique, from the décor to the furnishings. They also get, on average, more space and better value than a hotel, often enjoying things like kitchens or a suite-like setting, for a lower price. On the other hand, the host likes Airbnb because of the ease with which they can get started owning their own business, with just a few simple steps. Whereas opening a proper bed and breakfast could be an endeavor that takes years of work and tens of thousands of dollars, Airbnb allows you to get started with just a few simple steps.

The Next Practical Actions to Take

- Are you a regular Airbnb traveler? Why did you pick Airbnb? Write down the reasons why you picked Airbnb versus a hotel on various occasions. Were your expectations met? Why or why not?

- Do you have a friend who is an Airbnb host who would be willing to talk about their experience? (If not, chances are you have a social media friend who is one – put out a post and ask if any hosts will be willing to talk to you about their experience for fifteen minutes. You'd be surprised; people truly love to feel like an expert and talk about themselves. If you do this, make sure to be punctual and keep the call to the promised length of time. Use the following questions as a script.) Don't forget to take notes or ask permission to record the conversation. Ideally, you will speak to five people about their experiences in different cities with different kinds of properties.

- o How did you get started, and why?

- o Why do you think people like your property? What kinds of guests do you have?

- o What was your biggest challenge in getting started?

- o What would you do differently in getting started now?

- o What makes a successful host?

- o What have been your most rewarding aspects of the hosting experience?

- o Any drawbacks?

- o How are you able to increase numbers of bookings and obtain super host status?

- Do you have friends who have traveled using Airbnb? Following the same idea as above, ask five of them to talk with you about their experience. Ask them:

- o What do you look for in an Airbnb listing?

- o What makes a successful experience for you?

- o What does the average host forget to do that the excellent one remembers to do?

- o What makes you leave a five-star review?

- o What turns you off in a listing?

- o In what circumstances would you choose a hotel over an Airbnb listing? (certain cities, certain kinds of trips, etc.)

CHAPTER 2: WHY AIRBNB IS NOT THE SAME AS REAL ESTATE

Before getting started, it is crucial to know the differences between earning money through traditional real estate and through Airbnb listings, as well as the benefits, drawbacks, and misconceptions of the similarities between the two. Quite simply, by investing in traditional real estate, you are choosing to become a landlord, with all the benefits and drawbacks. It means you are looking for a tenant who will stay for the long term, usually for six months or more, and who will enter into a legal agreement with you personally about all the terms. (Note: while most of the discussion of being a landlord applies to the practice of subleasing a room within your leased apartment, there may be different rules, laws, and expectations in your individual community, so make sure to investigate them before trying to sublease. See this advice for more.)

While this book is not designed to teach you all the basics of being a landlord (see this comprehensive article for more), some basic things to keep in mind are the following:

A landlord must set the right tone with his tenants to ensure he gets paid every single month. While he might want to be "friendly," he also needs to be authoritative or risk losing money during the course of what will likely be a long-term relationship. He must be ready to drop everything to perform repairs (or hire a property manager), he must be aware of rental laws (for example, how much can rent be increased every year, and what are local eviction procedures) and then take out relevant insurance. Moreover, he must be savvy enough to set the rent at the right level – and to know that once the contract is signed, it becomes impossible to change the price during the term of the lease, and afterward only possible to raise the rent in small increments. Then he must advertise for, and select, the right tenant, making sure to do appropriate background and credit checks. As soon as he gets notice from a tenant who plans to leave, he must start the process again, organizing viewings of the property with potentially flaky new prospective tenants and coordinating the schedule with his current tenant – and if things do not go well, he risks having the property vacant for long periods of time, particularly if his rental market is tied to a university calendar and has dramatic ebbs and flows. Finally, the landlord will have to create a legal document to be signed by both him and the tenant, which may include additional requirements such as the fact that the tenant needs to acquire renter's insurance. The lease also needs to have terms regarding how eventual wear and tear to the property will be assessed, and how much deposit the tenant must give – and how it will be refunded (in accordance with local laws).

From the very start, Airbnb works in a diverse way, because of the technological platform that has been built to help put guests and hosts into contact and because of the short-term nature of the enterprise. To contrast real estate investments with Airbnb, first off, the tone of the relationship between the people is already established in the individual listing profiles each person sets. However, you can be as authoritative or laid back as you want, although it is easier to be slightly more laid back on Airbnb because you can rest assured that you will get paid – guests must pay by credit card at the time of booking, and your payment is released to you after their check-in, assuming that there are no major issues. Then, when you meet the guest (if you choose to), you will be presenting yourself as a friendly host, not as a landlord. This is a major consideration before becoming an Airbnb host: how comfortable you feel with people. Small talk matters and can be the difference between a four- and five-star review. If you are not a people person, you might prefer to be a landlord (or get a property manager), where the actual friendliness is not a major element of the relationship – or at least not a deal-breaker.

Compared to a landlord, the biggest outlay of time for the Airbnb host (after the actual preparation of the property) is the development of the online profile and listing. This includes taking high-quality photographs of the property (which has to be furnished), describing it and all its amenities, and laying out all the procedures, including house rules, check-in and check-out. In order to get a booking, the host simply has to wait to receive a message. If the host allows it, the guest may choose to instant book, which means that the entire transaction goes through without any necessary involvement of the host. If the guest wants to inquire, perhaps because he has an unusual request or just needs more information, the host receives a message from him and can engage in a back and forth. The host can choose to approve or decline the request and block the days the guest is interested in – or leave them available. Once the booking is made, the guest receives check-in information, and the host will have to prepare the space – either cleaning it himself or hiring a service. The host will receive the payment, the guest will check out, and if there is any damage, the host reports it and requests compensation (more on this in a subsequent chapter). Then the guest and host review one another, and the host prepares the property for the next guest. The host will have to keep up the property, making sure linens and towels are clean, the kitchen (if any) is stocked with whatever goodies they choose, and that everything is in generally good condition. That is basically the extent of it – a rather different experience from the landlord's because all the legal agreements and customer service issues are taken care of by the site.

There are, of course, some similarities between the two: hosts are allowed to screen their guests and can reject a guest who does not have a good rating or who has needs that cannot be met by their property. However, there are legal protections that apply in both cases. For example, just as landlords are required to allow service animals in their property in the case of a tenant who has a medical need, so too must Airbnb hosts – even if they have listed their property as animal-free. Then, an Airbnb host will also be responsible for any repair work that might need to be done. This can be a challenge when hosting multiple people, because if you want to coordinate between a guest and a repairman (who might not have a set schedule either), you may have to do a lot of back and forth via text message. While some more subtle repair issues might be able to be delayed in an Airbnb, in most cases you will have to be on the ball with them – a tenant might be patient if there is no hot water for a day, but a guest will be furious if they show up after a long day of traveling and find a cold shower.

A major difference, of course, is the issue of the length of the stay. While most landlords prefer tenants to sign a year or more contract, in order to avoid the possibility of having the property vacant, Airbnb hosts can often do better with shorter-term rentals: because each guest can be assessed a cleaning fee of the host's choosing, it is possible to make more money with more frequent, shorter stays, as opposed to a guest who books for an entire month. Furthermore, most hosts offer discounts for longer stays, eating into the profit margin – but decreasing the amount of time that must be spent turning over the property with each new guest.

Another major difference is the absolute flexibility with Airbnb versus real estate rentals. A host can choose to allow bookings as far in advance as he wants – or only in the immediate future. That means that if you are unsure about whether you will like the experience of renting, you do not have to commit for a long time at first (and you can always open up the calendar later on, once you have developed a sense of whether or not it is for you). In a worst-case scenario, even if you have future bookings, Airbnb allows you to cancel them – if, for instance, you decided you needed to quit immediately (for instance, if you own the property you are Airbnb-in and suddenly decided to sell it). This will give you a bad rating on the site, but it might be worth it, depending on the circumstances. In the world of rentals business, ending a lease would have to make you either convince (and pay off) the tenant, or you would have to take some sort of legal action, which is costly and time-consuming.

Finally, another major difference is the issue of pricing (see this expert perspective on flexible versus stable pricing). Airbnb is totally flexible, which means you can ask for more money on weekends, holidays, high tourist periods, and special events. You can lower your prices for mid-week and off-season days. This all means that your earnings are somewhat unknowable. They may well be higher than a regular rental, but you cannot guarantee what the amount will be per month. (If you have cash flow issues, however, it is great that the money comes in as it is earned so that you will have lots of smaller deposits distributed into your account over the month.) A rental, on the other hand, is more stable. Once you have the contract, you can count on the money – so it depends on how much appetite you have for risk.

Chapter Summary

If you are debating between whether to become a landlord or a real estate host, you have to take into consideration a number of factors, particularly in terms of your ability to handle the complex legal issues that arise when renting long term. This means educating yourself about the local laws in your area. You also have to decide whether you prefer a stable rent check (which might be a lower amount) or the possibly higher, but unpredictable amount that could come in from Airbnb. You also have to decide if you like working with people on a regular basis, if you are willing to take care of regular preparation of the property, and if you are willing and able to commit to renting for a longer period of time. If you just want to get your feet wet and you do not mind furnishing a property, the best way to go is Airbnb. Because there is no listing fee or commitment, you could even rent out your property one single time before deciding to do it again. You can also reprice your listing, rewriting your listing, or turn it over to a manager at any time. The choice is yours.

The Next Practical Actions to Take

Are you still unsure about renting (subleasing) or listing on Airbnb? It is a big decision, so we recommend that you try to get to know your local rental market by interviewing a rental agency – you could present yourself as a possible renter or possible landlord, and find out what you can expect in terms of a return on your investment. If you live in a community with a rental board, you could drop by their office or website and see what resources they provide for tenants and landlords, and inform yourself about local practices, such as rent control laws.

CHAPTER 3: GETTING THE CASH FLOWING: HOW MUCH TIME WILL YOU NEED TO COMMIT TO AIRBNB BEFORE YOU START MAKING A PROFIT

When you are about to start an exciting new business venture, one of your first questions will be: how soon can I see a return on my investment? Our answer? That depends. In the following chapter, we will lay out a few possible scenarios for timelines to profitability on Airbnb. None of these will be a replica of your unique, personal situation, (and we recommend that you be highly suspicious of anyone who promises you a cookie-cutter road map to profitability in any sector of any complexity whatsoever), but they will give you ideas about what to expect.

First, unless you already own or rent a property that can be used on Airbnb, you need to decide what geographical location to target to get started, and then start visiting properties. Depending on the heat of your local real estate market, and whether you decide to purchase or rent, this could take a few weeks or even a few months.

Next, you have to get the property up to the proper standards to give your guests a five-star experience. Again, depending on the state of the property, this might mean quick cosmetic things and fast trips to the hardware store and the local Ikea, or it might mean actually investing some time and money into the property if there are serious issues. A fresh coat of paint is always nice, as are thoughtful furnishings. As you prepare this stage of the process, remember, you do not need to be a perfectionist; you only need to get it into photograph ready condition: you can always return to fix the little details after you have posted the listing and are waiting for your first booking (as long as you do not leave yourself *too much* to get done, in case the first booking comes immediately).

Then it is time for photography. Did you know that Airbnb founders did market <u>research</u> to discover how good photography was one of the key ingredients of a successful listing? If you are not a very confident photographer, consider using Airbnb's service, available in many cities across the United States, in order to get high quality, affordable shots by photographers who know exactly what Airbnb guests want to see. This will cost you a little but will save you time.

Next, you have to design the listing, write all the rule books and then play the waiting game. Is it tourist season in your area? Are you lucky enough to live in an area that receives year-round visitors? This could be a major factor in how long it takes to get your first booking.

Once you get a booking, there is more waiting to be done – you have to have your first guest and, hopefully, get your first five-star review. Once you have a single review, things will speed up considerably, as future guests will feel more confident in trusting your listing.

The next step in speeding up the earnings process is to earn a super host rating, which you get by having a high percentage of five-star reviews over a certain period of time.

Now that we have outlined the timeline for earning money let us see what other hosts have to say about their experience. Remember, these are just examples:

This millennial <u>blogger</u> posted the experience of a friend of his, Jerry Xiong, a Super Host with nine listings in Columbus, OH. Mr. Xiong claims that he was able to gather over 500 five-star ratings and generate six figures of income within 2 years, spending minimal time and capital in the process. Another Airbnb host, <u>blogger,</u> and creator of the course "Hacking Airbnb," earn from $6,000 to $11,000 per month for his San Francisco apartment, with just about $3,500 in monthly expenses – after just two years of hosting experience. Thanks to his success in San Francisco, he decided to work on properties around the world, launching successful listings in Buenos Aires, Baltimore, Oakland, and small in Kansas.

Another couple that we interviewed in the Research Triangle in North Carolina was able to start earning their first thousand dollars within just five months of acquiring their first property – a small one-bedroom on the lower level of their home – easily making it to sixteen thousand their first year, and steadily increasing their profits to eighteen thousand in subsequent years. They are now are currently on track to earn twenty thousand this year, allowing them to cover the entire cost of their home expenses, simply by renting out a fraction of the available space.

Chapter Summary

Getting started on Airbnb is easier than you think, but it will require some upfront investment of time and money. Keep in mind that you need to create a welcoming space that will photograph well but does not waste too much time on perfecting it. Get your listing up there, and then while you are waiting, improve as necessary. (Pro tip: you can also solicit opinions from guests after they visit, asking them their opinions on your amenities before they leave a review. This will make them feel included – and generate useful ideas for how to improve your space in a way that customers actually desire.) While countless factors will influence exactly how long your path to profitability will take, it is possible to start earning money within a few months of planning out your strategy. A good estimate of how long it will take to start earning five figures, is about one to two years, depending on how heavily you invest in multiple properties.

The Next Practical Actions to Take

Unsure about how long it will take you to get your Airbnb running? Now is the time to outline your ideal deadlines to make sure you stay on track. Remember to consider:

1. How long it takes to secure a new property given the current conditions of your real estate market, your real estate goals, and

your desirability as a tenant or borrower. (If you have terrible credit or no reliable prior recommendations from past landlords, this step will take longer.)

Your Estimated Start Date:
Your Estimated End Date:

Your actual start date:
Your actual end date:

2. How long it takes you to bring the property up to standards

Your Estimated Start Date:
Your Estimated End Date:

Your actual start date:
Your actual end date:

3. How long it takes you to photograph the property

Your Estimated Start Date:
Your Estimated End Date:

Your actual start date:
Your actual end date:

4. How long it takes to get your first booking

Your Estimated Start Date:
Your Estimated End Date:

Your actual start date:
Your actual end date:

5. How long it takes to get your first rating

   Your Estimated Start Date:
   Your Estimated End Date:

   Your actual start date:
   Your actual end date:

If you keep a record of this here or in another designated spot, you can use it as a point of reference to track your progress – and to compare how much faster and more accurately you are able to progress on to your subsequent properties. Remember, investing in your learning curve is an investment in your future abilities to earn more money in a more efficient manner – which is the real goal of passive income.

CHAPTER 4: A BRIEF HISTORY OF AIRBNB

This chapter will briefly dive into the history of Airbnb and how the organization came about as well as some of the values behind it.

Airbnb is not just a cheap tourist alternative to hotels. It was founded by Brian Chesky and Joe Gebbia, who developed the company not simply to disrupt the hotel industry. Instead, they wanted to form a business that centered on providing tourists access to authentic local experiences. More than just a cheap alternative to a hotel room, the local experience and the encounter between the guest and host, was their primary interest in developing their business. The reason why the company was called Air Bed and Breakfast is a humorous reference to the fact that the founders used air mattresses on their apartment floor to host their first guests. They took advantage of a shortage in the hotel market in San Francisco, that caused all the hotel rooms to be fully occupied before a popular conference was to take place. They had the brilliant idea of renting four mattresses in their apartment – but beyond that, they also gave their guests breakfast and showed them around town.

When the 2008 Democratic National Convention came to Denver in 2008 and the hotel market was once again inundated with requests, the men were able to gain traction. They had designed an online website to help locals rent out their rooms to the people attending the convention. Thanks to their success, they won a spot in a startup accelerator known as Y Combinator, that is celebrated across the world. They also took the opportunity to travel the country and meet their early hosts, teaching them what made a great listing (which is why we recommend you do the same kind of market research). Throughout their development, however, the main value that Airbnb founders stressed is the importance of community. They learned this as they pushed the growth of their business by using word of mouth before having the traction required to rely on more conventional marketing methods. This meant that hosts would share with other potential hosts the benefits of their experience and that travelers would also spread the word about the extraordinary new way of traveling to a different city.From four air mattresses in a single apartment to 38 billion dollars – the Airbnb story is nothing short of impressive, and you can be a part of it too.

Chapter Summary

As with any venture, it is important to know about the industry you are investing in – this will prepare to you avoid any unpleasant surprises and to know how to make the most of your investment. In the case of Airbnb, although the company and its technology are relatively young, it has a good track record, especially when it comes to lobbying for its survival when cities and towns try to regulate or ban it. Specifically, when looking at the history of Airbnb, the story of its founding puts a lot of emphasis on the community aspect of hosting and traveling, so it is essential to keep that value in mind when deciding whether to join the community.

The Next Practical Actions to Take

Ready to take the plunge? If you have a financial planner, now might be a good time to sit down with him or her in order to discuss your intentions, understand how much available cash you have, and figure out an ideal timeline for the venture. You might also use this stage in the planning process to figure out alternative investment options and what the expected returns on those investments might be. You could look at other online rental sites, like Vacation Rentals by owner (or even do a comparison with long term renting, as discussed in chapter two), or try other kinds of income investments like dividend stocks. By making a side by side comparison of projected earnings, you can be more confident in the decision you are making, if you ultimately choose to go for the Airbnb hosting venture. Do not forget to factor in the value of your own time when making the calculations.

CHAPTER 5: WHAT YOU NEED TO KNOW BEFORE YOU START MAKING YOUR MONEY

Airbnb hosting is not for everyone, and it is not the kind of purely passive investment where you literally sit around, and your money grows. This chapter will go through the main challenges you will need to face when building your Airbnb business in order to be best prepared to face them when they occur.

Personal elements

As discussed in chapter one, a primary reason why people like Airbnb is because of the human connection. As nice as your hotel concierge might treat you during your few minutes of interaction, you rarely would feel like you are getting to know an actual person – there is always the element of the employee-client relationship at work. The Airbnb experience is all about the guest host dynamic, and this means you will have to be comfortable speaking to strangers of all kinds: people who want to talk of your ear, people who complain about phantom smells, people who text you constantly for every tiny question, people whose politics you do not agree with, and people who break the rules (or your things). Sure, you will meet many lovely people and the majority of your guests will be fairly neutral, but you have to be prepared for tough personalities and know how to handle them.

When you start your Airbnb, unless you have a property management company involved from the outset, you will also be on the clock. This means getting the apartment ready in time for your guests, especially when there is a tight turnaround time between check-in and check-out. It means being available to answer requests whenever they come in (Airbnb will rate you based on how quickly you answer, so stay in reach of a phone), and it means being ready to handle any issues that arrive, whether its maintenance or a hospitality request. If a guest asks you for a toothbrush because they forgot theirs, you should be ready to bring one over for them immediately – or risk losing points on your review!

There are a few other personal qualities that are required for being a successful Airbnb host, that are important to consider before deciding whether to take the plunge. When you first start hosting, you will need to make sure you are good working with time constraints. This includes every aspect of the process, starting with the app: you will need to install it on your phone and check it regularly, as you will soon start to get booking requests and inquiries, and if you do not reply promptly, you risk losing the booking or getting the relationship off on the wrong step. (Airbnb will also dock you points if you do not reply within twenty-four hours of an inquiry, which will adversely affect your ability to get and maintain the coveted super host status.)

Then whenever you have a guest on your property – and this will become exponentially important if you get to the point of having multiple properties – you also have to be ready to respond to requests at the drop of a hat. What happens if they get locked out? Where is the backup the key? What happens if there is a problem accessing the space during check-in? Even if you have a property management company in place, you are still the boss, and they may have to be in touch with you for certain things. For instance, if they need to make a repair or purchase above a certain dollar amount, they will have to notify you, as per your contract – and until you reply, they will not be able to move on the repair, which could, in turn, affect the quality of the guest's experience. Imagine you have a mountain property where the access is determined by a long private driveway, and a tree falls in a storm: if you are not on top of that accident, either calling the tree removal company yourself or approving the expense with the managers, your guest could be trapped in dangerous conditions. So be prepared for the worst to happen, and make sure you are ready to handle whatever may come.

Another important quality for a successful host is the ability to manage expectations. Remember, Airbnb gives you the platform, but you are your own marketer on the site. The way you craft your profile, the way you interact with any guest – from the very first inquiry – will set the tone. Is your house a party zone? Great, use fun language on the site. Do you need it quiet to keep the peace with your neighbors? Okay, well spell that out on the site as well. In cases where you know that there is some aspect of the property that might annoy some people, it's best to be upfront, either in your description or in a private message after they book. One example of this is if the property is in an apartment building with tenants above them. Will, the guests, hear footsteps and maybe voices, perhaps at inconvenient hours? Let them know so they are not furious when they are woken up at six am. Is there a shared wall with a bakery, where the clatter of dishes and the whir of espresso machines will be going all day? Make that clear. If the property is a shared space, expectations have to be very clearly managed from the outset. If there are rules about which spaces can be accessed and when, make sure to let the guest know – or face their anger. Maybe these words of advice sound straightforward to you – if so, great. But if you're the kind of person who beats around the bush, think hard before you become an Airbnb host, because that is the kind of attitude that might get you in trouble.

Business elements

After considering the personal ingredients necessary for being an amazing Airbnb host, it is important to consider the business elements of successful hosting. First, you will need to understand the risks and liabilities involved in becoming a host, particularly if you do not own the property. In order to mitigate these risks, you will have to be able to build rapport and negotiate with potential landlords, in order to keep the relationship smooth. You will have to investigate the insurance requirements for Airbnb hosts. Moreover, as you assess the risks involved, you will have to take into account the current local market conditions.

Then, in terms of the economics of the endeavor, you will have to make several decisions, including how much to charge for the different properties you list. This will also include extra fees for additional guests beyond a set number, as well as a cleaning fee and how much you want to keep as a deposit. You will also have to decide how to position the business: who are you catering to? What kind of guests would you prefer to avoid? (Without being caught for discrimination, which is forbidden on Airbnb.)

Why One Platform?

Earlier in the book, we mentioned other rental sites. VRBO.com is the most prominent alternative to Airbnb, and there are also no-frills sites such as Craigslist that function simply as an electronic bulletin board. Booking.com is another competitor, but it offers much fewer services than Airbnb, asking hosts to do more work.

We mentioned studying other alternatives and deciding on one of them before getting started. But why not multiply your chances of success by using more than one site? Because Airbnb was designed to be the only site that you use, and it rewards you – handsomely – for doing so. First, on a practical level, Airbnb keeps your calendar straight for you, so you do not have to worry about double booking. Nothing puts off guests and spreads bad word of mouth more than canceling a booking because of a mistake in your calendar. Airbnb also allows instant booking, a feature that many guests prefer, and if you have multiple sites in play, you will have to turn off that feature in order to avoid deadly double bookings, costing you in the long run. The other main reason why it is important to focus just on one platform like Airbnb as opposed to several is that it is better for things like reviews. With each guest who gives you a review, you are amassing a valuable asset. True, it is an asset that cannot be transferred to any other platform (for instance, if one day Airbnb collapses), but this is a case in which it is better to put your eggs in one basket. If you try to get a good reputation on multiple sites, it will take way longer, and you may never reach the coveted and lucrative super host status.

Why You Should First Get to Know Airbnb as a Guest

If you have never traveled using Airbnb, we highly recommend you do so now, even if it is just for one night in a nearby city (or even your own city!). Why you may ask? For several reasons: first, because being an Airbnb guest will help you build up your personal rating, which will be a big help when you make your first listing and have not yet gotten a five-star review from a guest. Second, because being a guest will enable you to start to learn about what other hosts do well – and what you think they should not do – in order to be successful. If you already know what kind of property you want, absolutely try to stay at similar kinds of properties (if you want to be renting a single room, for example, make it a priority to try that kind of house.) Regardless, try to stay at a variety of kinds of listings, as each different highly-rated property will have something to spark your imagination.

Who is Getting Richest through Airbnb?

Recent data provided by Airbnb suggests that the demographic group that makes the most money in hosting is older women. According to one successful <u>host</u>, this is because of two key reasons, one practical and one psychological: they tend to be property owners, and they tend to be nurturers who know how to make guests feel welcome. Now, if you are an older woman reading this, great, you are in a good position to start making significant money on Airbnb. If not, no worries – of course! – Plenty of other demographics can be successful and, honestly, as useful as demographics are for predicting large trends, all you really need to worry about is *you*. So, keep the lesson in mind – nurturing hosts (as long as they are not overbearing or intrusive) tend to be more successful.

Chapter Summary

Since Airbnb hosting is not for everyone (although it does appear to be a great possibility for older women in particular), this chapter went through the main personal and business challenges you might have to face when growing your new business. This includes:

- being comfortable speaking to strangers
- working well with time constraints
- knowing how to manage expectations
- understanding the risks and liabilities involved
- knowing how to build rapport and negotiate with landlords
- learning about the kinds of insurance policies available
- knowing how to set your price
- positioning the business to target the ideal demographic
- assessing local market conditions

The chapter ended with some important information on why you should only concentrate on one platform (to avoid double bookings and maximize reviews), why you should stay at other Airbnb's before trying to become a host (to get good reviews as a guest and to learn more about what makes a good host), and who makes the most money on Airbnb (older women who are good at nurturing their guests).

Next Practical Actions to Take

- Sit down with a trusted friend and go through the list of important traits in a host. Do a personality assessment and see how you measure up.

- Start visiting another Airbnb's. Make sure to be a good guest by reading the rule book, leaving the space neat when you check out and communicating promptly with the hosts so that you get five-star ratings from your host in order to start building up your profile. During your stay, take notes on what you like and don't like about each space. Ask yourself what little touches made your stay special? (Free coffee? Nice quality linens? A welcome note?) Note: If you cannot currently afford to take multiple vacations, you could also contact hosts and see if it is possible to view a place that you are considering renting on behalf of a friend. They might say no, but they might say yes!

CHAPTER 6: SO HOW DO YOU MAKE MONEY WITHOUT OWNING A HOME?

How to use retail arbitrage on Airbnb

While the more traditional path to becoming an Airbnb, the host is by renting out your own home or part of it, or another property of yours, with a concept known as "Airbnb rental arbitrage" you can make money without owning your own home. In business terms, arbitrage means that you buy something cheap and sell it for more money, and to do so at the same time, in order to make a profit. The difference between cost and earnings is profit. In practical terms, this means you rent an apartment and then sublet it to other Airbnb guests. As long as the revenue from the short term's rental is more than the cost of renting (as well as furnishing and managing the property), you are succeeding at Airbnb rental arbitrage.

What to do when landlords reject you

If the landlord says no, the best way to handle the situation is to be respectful and to ask if you may speak to their legal counsel (or find out who they are on your own)– not to be adversarial, of course, but to see if they can do something to present your case more effectively. Lawyers have a job to work in their client's best interest, so if you can show them that you have a way for the landlord to make money and are not breaking any laws, then they are required to present it to the landlord for you. If his or her own legal counsel says, "This is legal and it can work," it becomes much more difficult for a landlord to reject you.

What are the costs and timeframes involved?

Example of costs: if you can rent an apartment in your area for $1000 per month (including utilities), and you can rent furnishings for another $200 per month. To make a profit, you only need to earn more than $1200 per month. If you can rent out your apartment for $100 per night, after you deduct the 3% service fee that Airbnb charges hosts, then you would need to have guests in the unit for 12 nights out of the month to break even. If you were able to have guests lease the apartment for 30 nights, then you would make $1,800 in profit. Do not forget that if you prefer to pay someone to manage or clean the place, then you will need to deduct that from your costs as well. (Cleaning costs can be recuperated by charging them directly to the guest as an add on fee.)

The timeframe for Airbnb rental arbitrage is, unfortunately, one of the things that are least in your control. Since you are asking the landlord for something, you are on his or her timeline. In order to speed this up, you can be proactive and send reminders, and you can visit multiple properties if you are searching around for a new landlord with whom to do business. But in this situation, patience is a virtue. You want your landlord to want to do business with you, not to be annoyed at your pesky attitude.

What are the regulations around Airbnb?

Airbnb has a number of useful articles on their website to discuss the relevant regulatory issues you should look into before hosting on Airbnb. As you can see from a brief summary below, they decline to provide specific information on individual cities and counties, as there are so many different variables – which change with frequency. This would make it impractical to detail them all in one spot. Below are the main issues you need to know about and inform yourself of, in regard to your desired location.

- **Business Licenses**: in some cities, owners must apply for before they can start running their business. See your local government website for information.

- **Building and Housing Standards**: there may be local and state regulations that set the standards for the quality of a building that is to be rented, in terms of its health and safety (for example, this could be a requirement that there be a bathroom available or electricity and running water). In some cases, you might even need to get your property inspected officially in order to rent it out. Check the website of your local government to find out what rules are applicable to your desired listing.

- **Zoning Rules**: cities and counties may also have laws that determine the way that you are allowed to use your home. Make sure to check these rules to see if you are allowed to rent your property on Airbnb. Or contact your local government directly.

- **Special Permit**: in less often cases, some cities or counties can require a special permit to rent out your home. See your local government website to see if one is necessary and how to apply for one.

- **Taxes**: In many cases, cities, counties, and states make hosts collect a tourism tax for every overnight guest, and then pay that tax to the city or county. Contact your local government to see if you need to collect any taxes. (In some cases, Airbnb has made arrangements to collect and pay the taxes directly on your behalf – they will notify you, if so. But if not, you will be responsible for doing that.)

- **Other Rules**: There are lots of other potential rules if you have a lease, so make sure to read that document carefully. Other rules might influence the ability to rent out timeshares, or properties like condos and co-ops. If you have a Home Owners Association (HOA) or a tenant organization, these groups will also have by-laws that you should carefully consult for language addressing house-sharing agreements.

Chapter Summary

Retail arbitrage is a great way to earn money on Airbnb without owning a home. Obviously, you have to be smart about it and approach your landlord with confidence and knowledge about your situation. If they are at all hesitant, especially if you live in a hot real estate market, you will likely have to offer a percentage of the profits or to pay a little more rent – but it will be worth it, in the end, if you manage to secure their permission. Before getting started, however, make sure you have checked into all the local regulations. This will also prepare you when going to talk to the landlord, in case they are worried about the legality of the situation.

Next Practical Actions to Take

- Have you already picked the location or property you want to list? Do your due diligence and investigate the different regulations your city or county might have. Are short term rentals allowed? What are the regulations for business owners?

CHAPTER 7: MONEY MONEY

This chapter will cover the exact amount of money you will need to invest in Airbnb and discuss how you need to have a business mindset to succeed.

When it comes to money, there is good news and bad news. The bad news is, we cannot tell you how much money you need to invest in Airbnb. Here is the good news: depending on where you live and what kind of property you want to list, you can invest almost any amount of money in Airbnb to get started.

Take the following examples:

1. The cheapest option: You want to rent out your guest bedroom, which is already furnished. In this case, you need to make the following investments:

    o Permission from the landlord, if renting, which might include some percentage of your earnings, an increased security deposit or a small increase in rent.

    o An extra set of house keys from the hardware store (a few bucks)

    o A professional cleaning for the house (or does it yourself), which could be anywhere from $50 - $300

    o Photography – do it yourself, or pay Airbnb's photographers a small fee ($100)

That is, it, $500 tops. Now, of course, your return on the investment will also be smaller, as you cannot list a shared room for as much as private property, but it gives you an idea about how to get your feet wet.

2. A moderate/expensive option: you want to get an entire property to rent out.

- o If you are using arbitrage, that means laying out 1-3 month's rent to the landlord (this could range anywhere from $500 - $6000, depending on where you are located and how much money they want upfront). If you are buying it, it means 20 percent down payment, plus closing costs, which could range from the tens to hundreds of thousands of dollars.

- o Furnishing the apartment: this will depend on how big it is and whether you want to go thrifty or Ikea or high end, so this could also range from $2000 for a studio to $5000 or more for a bigger property. Some cities also have furniture rentals, if you cannot layout a lot of cash up front, but this will be more expensive in the long run, and you will have to be more careful about dealing with damages.

- o Outfitting the apartment: you might also need appliances if you have a kitchen or kitchenette, and you will also want bedding and decorations — $ 500 to $1000.

- o Security and related gadgets: count on a few hundred dollars for these useful gadgets.

- o Do not forget to add everything from above, including keys, cleaning, and photography.

- o You will also have to check with your insurance provider to see if you need a supplemental policy.

- o Don't forget to look into town and county rules about any necessary permits or taxes, which could cost you money.

- o Do you have to add anything to the property to make it competitive? Is that something you can do later? (For example, a hot tub in a ski area.)

Once you get a bigger property, you can see how the costs become much more unpredictable. Other chapters will cover how to make decisions about gadgets and furnishing.

A Business Mindset

Now that things are getting more real, remember what got you motivated to start doing this Airbnb in the first place. Yes, it might be painful to think about risking your cash. Yes, you will have to start out by spending, and it might take a little while for the balance to be back in the positive, but if you do all the suggested practical actions we recommend, you should feel confident that you are on the right path to make your money back quickly. Having a business mindset and recognizing that it is necessary to spend money in order to make money will be one of the biggest keys to success in your Airbnb hosting experience. This is what will distinguish you from the competition and allow you to supplement income and eventually even replace your day job. Otherwise, you may be stuck in your dreary office for the rest of your life, living paycheck to paycheck, vacation to vacation, weekend to weekend, just like your parents did.

Chapter Summary

Although it is impossible to state exactly how much money is needed to start an Airbnb, depending on your goals and needs – and what you have available to you – you can start Airbnb for almost no money at all. Or you can plunge a lot of cash into the endeavor. The important thing is that you are smart with how much you invest, and only invest a lot when you know that you are committed to this course of action. You also must figure out the appropriate amount to invest based on what you can recoup and how soon you need to recoup the investment. If you blow $10,000, will it take you a year to get that back? Is that okay with you? The worst thing to do is to go into this blindly, so make sure you have a detailed financial plan. While you might think you have to spend more to earn more, it is not always a one to one ratio. The goal is to study the market and find your sweet spot.

Next Practical Actions to Take

o Now is the time to make your financial calculations, as you figure out how much you can spend to get your business off the
ground, and how long you expect it will take to earn it back. This
means looking at things like how much rentals cost in your area
and what Airbnb's of comparable size can charge.

o Do you have a business mentor? If so, try talking to that person
about any doubts you are having. They likely once had them too!

CHAPTER 8: RENTING, OWNING, AND LANDLORD NEGOTIATION

Many potential hosts approach Airbnb rental arbitrage with a nonchalant attitude, thinking their landlord will not care what they do with the property, if things are quiet, and the rent is paid. In fact, some people think they are not even obliged to tell the landlord, let alone ask them. While it might seem quicker to just fly under the radar, this website has great guidelines for approaching a landlord, that will help you navigate a smooth relationship and assure you never face a potential blow up that could leave you facing eviction.

Step one, make sure you understand your landlord's point of view: he is likely working as a landlord in order to get a low risk but relatively small influx of cash. Their risk includes losing a tenant and needing to find another one, having to evict a tenant, and facing property damage – all of which can be handled relatively easily. So, imagine that you are a property owner who has put in a lot of effort to making the property livable. Their goal is to sign a tenant for a long contract and then sit back and collect their checks, spending as little time or effort as possible (which, although expected, only detracts from their profits). Now try to envision your tenant making a request: to allow many strangers to sleep in their property for his own personal profit. That request just changed the equation in the landlord's mind. Instead of low risk and modest income, they still have the same modest income but now have a high risk on their hands.

One of the biggest risks faced by a landlord who is renting through Airbnb is that it could put their homeowner's insurance in jeopardy because it means that their dwelling is being used as a business, not as a home. Other risks include more damage to the property and the fact that many cities forbid and even fine short-term rentals, which your landlord would be on the hook for. The best way to mitigate this increase in risk is to offer your landlord something in return.

In order to have the best possible outcome, prepare for a conversation with a landlord. Think about your position as a tenant (how long have you been a tenant, or are you a new potential tenant? How good of a tenant are you? How strong is your rental market / how easy would it be for your landlord to replace you? Would other tenants be influenced?). Then think about what you can offer the landlord, whether it is to extend your lease, pay more per month, or pre-pay months of rent.

One blogger proposes another possibility, a middle ground when dealing with landlords: when discussing the terms of the lease, try to negotiate a lower monthly rental price with the landlord in exchange for sharing profits with them. If the rental unit you are looking at costs $1,000 per month. You could ask them for a $700 rate in exchange for 20 percent or 30 percent of the profit from your guest bookings. This not only helps protect you in case of slower months and gives you a little extra cash to get the property ready; it also puts you in a collaborative relationship with the landlord. This means that they are much more likely to be more supportive about repairs and other incidentals if he is profiting too. Do not forget to get any agreement in writing to ensure a smooth relationship.

Finally, think about reassurances you can give the landlord, including the $1,000,000 Airbnb host guarantee; the possibility of purchasing your own vacation rental insurance; the possibility of limiting rentals to certain groups and times; agreeing to be present at all times (if this is possible); offering to change your contract to promise that you will cover certain kinds of damage; offering to give a bigger security deposit. You could also offer to be responsible for covering repairs up to a certain dollar amount.

The Differences between Owning and Renting Your Airbnb

The big difference between owning and renting your Airbnb is in the amount of freedom and responsibility you have. If you own your property, you can be free to make whatever modifications you want. You can be less worried about your neighbors (although always try to be respectful, just to keep things easy). You also must take care of all repairs, but you can do them on your terms.

If you rent, you will have to be more creative in how you deal with space. You cannot just upgrade a cheap fridge or rip up the carpet. You also have to be constantly peacekeeping with the neighbors and with your landlord so that nothing unpleasant happens. It is mostly common sense, so if you are a good tenant, you should soon get the hang of things as a host.

Chapter Summary

The talk with the landlord is what most people fear when getting ready to do Airbnb rental arbitrage, but prepare yourself to use these guidelines, and you will likely be off to a great start.

Next Practical Actions to Take

- Do you already have a specific rental property in mind? Get prepared to talk to your landlord by asking yourself:
  - How strong is my position as a tenant?
  - What is the landlord's state of mind? (Are they a big thinker/entrepreneur? Conservative?)
  - How can I best put myself in my landlord's position to help them see things from my perspective?
  - What can I offer my landlord? (A bigger security deposit, a longer lease, a percentage of the profits, a higher monthly rent, new language in the lease to agree to cover certain damage.)
  - What is my plan b if the landlord says no?

CHAPTER 9: TIME TO DIVE IN

In order to get started, you need to know how much to charge. The first place where prospective hosts should research pricing is on the Airbnb website itself. Search your local area and see what other people are charging for a given night. This will give you a general idea of what you can expect, as anything wildly outside this range will fail to gain traction. The Airbnb automatic pricing tool will also give you professional suggestions based on their analytics. However, if you want a third party, professional-grade tool, we recommend you check out AirDNA, a platform that has both free and subscription-based options, and that provides valuable insight into pricing and competition.

The AirDNA tools for Airbnb hosts promise to allow you to outperform the competition by helping you easily to compare short term rentals in your chosen market. With an interactive map, the MarketMinder tool lets Airbnb hosts see what comparable vacation rentals are charging. You can zoom all the way down into neighborhoods and find out possible daily rates, average occupancy, and annual revenue expectations. (This is a fabulous tool during your budgeting phases as well as during your immediate ramp-up to launching.) The tool also offers a way to dynamically price your listings through an interactive calendar that displays seasonal trends (excellent for identifying and preparing yourself for a low season.) You can also learn about your ideal average daily rate and use supply and demand charts that predict how prices fluctuate seasonally. You can even use an interactive calendar to show what is likely to happen to your revenue depending on how much you charge. Finally, AirDNA allows you to maximize your revenue by helping you to analyze the approach of local properties that are most competitive. This tool lets you get a sense of how often short-term vacation rentals are viewed, what their average ratings are, and what amenities they most commonly provide. You will be able to see who is earning the most and what they are charging and when. With that information in hand, you can find new potential investments and make the most of the ones you have.

Chapter Summary

Airbnb has some free tools built into the platform to help you understand how much to price your property and how to adjust the calendar pricing for high and low demand. However, if you do not just want to rely on them, and you have a little extra cash to invest, try AirDNA to get thorough information on competitors' pricing and suggestions about your own. Particularly if you are going to get multiple properties and invest heavily, you should not just trust your own casual searches of Airbnb but get real hard data in order to back up your decision.

Next Practical Actions to Take

- Search the Airbnb website for comparable listings in your area. Don't forget to put in various dates for travel to see how prices vary on weekends and weekdays and in different seasons during the year. Airbnb will also let you know if there are very few homes available during a certain time, so you can see if the area is overcrowded or has room for competition.

- Get on the AirDNA website, check out their offerings, try a free subscription and see if the paid options are worth it to you!

CHAPTER 10: WHAT CAN AFFECT YOUR LISTING

There are several factors that can affect your listing that you should keep an eye on. First, your listing details are incredibly important as they set the terms of the rental and whether it is attractive for a guest. Then, you should be turned into the guest's trip details and preferences, which you can learn about while you are hosting, as these will start to become apparent in real-time. Price, of course, is a major factor that can affect your listing – in fact, if your pricing is too far off average pricing, you will be severely limited in your ability to attract guests. Being a super host is a major factor in how your listing is perceived, as it serves as a guarantee of excellence that makes people more likely to trust you.

These factors together will affect your listing visibility, which Airbnb determines with a secret algorithm. The higher you rank on the search page, the better your chances of getting booked. Then, of course, your guest's experience and their review will be essential in affecting your listing. No one wants to stay at a place that is constantly being rated poorly.

Chapter Summary

If you keep on top of your listing details, guest preferences, pricing, super host status, and your reviews, you will earn higher visibility in the Airbnb search results and, thus, get more bookings.

Next Practical Actions to Take

- Answer the following questions
  - What stands out to you in another people's listing?
  - How does your listing compare?
  - Which of these areas do you need to improve on?

CHAPTER 11 - SO ARE YOU READY TO FURNISH?

This chapter will discuss how to decorate your Airbnb, which is an incredibly popular topic for Youtubers. (See, for example, this popular video.)

The first thing you need to decide is what your target demographic is, and then you need to consult either magazines or social media feeds that match that demographic. If you are going for a younger group, you want to find modern furniture, whereas if you want to go for an older demographic, especially for business travelers, you might want to go the stylish route – although be careful not to go over the top!

The second thing you need to decide is what your budget is and how long you hope to make the furniture last on that budget. (For example, if you just need to get started and are short on cash, you might want to use cheap furniture and then replace it with expensive furniture when you are more liquid – but that strategy might backfire as it might look cheap to guests or, worse, get destroyed quickly.)

Decoration tips:

A more expensive way to decorate your place is by changing the paint color in different rooms. Of course, you could also paint the place yourself, but then that will cost you time. Room color, especially a bold accent wall, can help your photos pop on the search page. A well-placed mirror can also make a room look bigger and, if positioned opposite a window can fill the space with light.

It's okay if you use your local Ikea for the bulk of your stuff, but try to get a few original pieces, even from a local thrift shop, just to make sure you have an original feel to your place.

Bedroom: Get the biggest bed you can fit in your space and have a range of different weight blankets for people to choose from. Have a nightstand on each side of the bed with a reading light and charging station. Bedrooms should have carpet or rugs, and make sure your closets have hangers.

Bathroom: This is where you can have some fun, with colorful shower curtains, matching cups, tissue box cover and towels.

Living room: make sure you have plenty of comfortable seating, including the biggest couch that fits and an additional love seat if possible. Make sure to have a place for guests to set down drinks while watching TV.

Kitchen: if you don't have an island with bar stools where guests can eat, make sure you have a kitchen table that's expandable and some extra folding chairs.

Special areas: one of the biggest selling points of an Airbnb is relaxing outdoor space that makes the guest feel like they are in another world. Or, if that is not in the realm of possibility for your current property, even a little outdoor area with a well-chosen aesthetic, can make a world of difference. For example, think about getting a set of table and chairs to put outside the house, if space permits (if you do not have a patio area, it is cheap and easy to install on with stone or brick). Pick fashionable (and washable!) cushions for the chairs and decorate the area with Christmas lights or a welcoming sign.

Don't forget outside details, like a doormat, which will make your guests more conscientious about wiping their feet before entering! Something quirky, like a metal lawn sculpture, can make your listing stand out (of course, you have to choose these details in concert with your target demographic, so be deliberate and coherent in your choices).

Chapter Summary

Furnishing a place is like your own personal touch that can make your Airbnb stand out. Photos are important, but you have to have something worthy of photography!

Next Practical Actions to Take

- Check out the countless online videos about decorating your Airbnb. Other good places to look for ideas include Pinterest boards. This could also be a good way to get to know design bloggers that feature Airbnb's. Maybe one day they will feature yours!

- Draw up a list of your main rooms, the big items you need for each one, and then the accessories you will need to make it all come together.

- If you are not good at designing, you may want to invest in a professional designer. There are low-cost ones available, that can work with standard items such as Ikea, and can work remotely.

CHAPTER 12: THE ESSENTIAL GADGET LIST

Everyone loves their gadgets, and a good Airbnb host will make use of new technological developments in order to make their job easier. At the same time, there is the added benefit that these gadgets can make guests feel comfortable and safe – and to make their listing eco-friendlier (and to save on electricity, too!). Remember, many of your guests might be repeat guests, and a little extra thoughtful gadget could make the difference for a guest who is trying to decide whether to come back or not.

The prestigious technology review website CNET.com, has the following <u>recommendations</u>:

1. Smart speakers (these are now cheap enough that if someone steals them, it is not a big deal, and it provides a nice amenity for people as they are settling in.)

2. Smart locks (this will allow you to do remote check-in and check-out and not worry about guests copying keys.)

3. Video doorbell (this will allow you to monitor if guests try to bring in extra guests)

   One <u>blogger</u> discusses his experience with a <u>Ring Video Door-bell</u>, which is a doorbell, security camera, and walkie-talkie combined. When somebody rings it (or even approaches the door unannounced), the owner gets an alert on his phone that can connect to a video feed of what is happening, allowing him to see anyone approaching or entering the premises.

4. Smart thermostat (if a guest checks out without turning down the heat or shutting the ac, you can do this remotely).

5. Smart lights (this is a great way to save electricity and also make yourself look fancy.)

6. Media streamer (everyone loves entertainment, especially when traveling.)

7. Security camera (just to make sure everything goes okay, and to have evidence in case something goes wrong.)

8. Motion sensors (to add additional security to the property.)

9. Charging station (most guests will have these, but it is very nice to have a back-up.)

Other ideas from the YourPorter* blog include:

1. Noise detector (if you are sensitive about noise in your listing, or your neighbors are, a noise detector can allow you to monitor noise remotely so that you deal with the problem before the neighbors do!)

2. Wireless charger (this is a fancy gadget that will be sure to impress your tech-savvy guests, allowing them to charge their devices without USB).

(*Note YourPorter is a subscription app that you can use to manage your Airbnb more seamlessly, including automatically sending out messages to guests, syncing your calendar, and coordinating team members.)

Gadgets to avoid anything invaluable or fragile! Most guests are not likely to steal from you but don't tempt them with something expensive. It is better to avoid any potential unpleasant events.

Chapter Summary

There are lots of inexpensive gadgets that can make your hosting experience better, safer, and more ecological, so check out the list we provide and see what works for you.

Next Practical Actions to Take

- Using the list, we provide, write a list of your own and decide which of these gadgets to prioritize and how much you are willing to spend on them.

CHAPTER 13: LET'S GET SOME INSURANCE

Insurance is an important part of Airbnb and is a complicated issue. First, all hosts should know the difference between the <u>Airbnb host guarantee</u> versus <u>Airbnb host protection insurance</u>. The *guarantee* is for damage to property, and the *protection insurance* is for a guest's personal injury. Both kinds are for damages up to $1,000,000, and hosts receive it for every stay that is booked. There is also coverage extended to some shared common spaces and for HOAs that might also get hit with a lawsuit. There are some exceptions to these policies, so go on the Airbnb site and read them carefully. They may also change from time to time, so stay updated.

Then you might want to get additional insurance, depending on where you live and what your personal attitude towards risk is. The best thing to do is to call your insurance agent and explain that you want to do home sharing. Ask for specific language in the policy that addresses home sharing and finds out if you need vacation rental insurance or business insurance. Some companies might not yet have policies as Airbnb is relatively new. Make sure to get multiple quotes to be sure you are getting the best deal.

Chapter Summary

In the unlikely event of severe injury or damage, your first line of defense for the property is the Airbnb host guarantee, and for personal injury, the host insurance. Then if you are more risk-averse, you can also make sure you are insured personally through your homeowners or renter's insurance.

Next Practical Actions to Take

- Read the Airbnb policies thoroughly, so you know what to expect

- Call several insurance agents to see what you should do about your personal coverage.

CHAPTER 14: HOW TO CREATE A KICK-ASS LISTING

Now that you've done all the groundwork, it is time to create a powerful listing. The goal is to rank number one on Airbnb searches for your area, but that will only come with time, as the ranking algorithm looks for a combination of factors that are not possible to achieve overnight.

The Airbnb listing starts with a short title that should be very catchy so that your description stands out above everyone else's. This is where you can set the tone, being funny if you want to appeal to kids, etc. What is the most important detail of your listing? That it is clean? Quiet? Those are nice, but maybe it is better to stress that it is close to a certain attraction, or that there is some funky detail that guests will love. Remember, they will likely be searching with a keyword like "Disney" or "stadium" or the name of the local university, so include a smart term in your title. A bad Airbnb title will sound just like everyone else's, using generic words like "best" or "awesome." while a good one will make the guest feel they are getting something unique and rare. Don't forget; the picture will be below, so you need to make the picture and title dialogue with one another to make the most effective.

The next part of the listing is the summary, and in five hundred words you need to highlight the best features of your listing. Always lead with the thing's guests need to know most: basic amenities and location of the property. But make sure to highlight any special attractions that your place provides, if it's a romantic getaway or an adventure, or a place for silent meditation.

The sections on Guest access and interactions are important for setting expectations: will you be an involved host, or will they never meet you? Make this clear so that there are no misunderstandings.

As you plan your listing, you want to keep in mind different Airbnb strategies: what are the main strengths of your listing? Do you want to make it exclusive and expensive (and have lower occupancy) or more economical and accessible and have higher occupancy?

Your listing will also have reviews, once you get some, and remember, only the first review will show on the initial page, so it is important to have a good one!

Another way you can improve the order your listing appears is by appearing on people's wish lists. You can do this by having a great listing, but you also can ask friends and family (and previous guests) to add you to their list, since it doesn't cost them anything.

You can also limit guests in terms of how many days they can stay, maximum and minimum. Think carefully about this – minimum stays are useful if you want to ensure that you don't get a random Saturday night stay that ruins a whole weekend, or if you don't want to constantly clean the apartment between guests. But in the low season, you might want to consider having no minimum. Maximum stays are good if you want to make sure you have turned over. This is useful because it will get you more reviews, which will improve your rating. Airbnb now lets you add a seasonal requirement to the min/max days of residence, for example, requiring a weeklong stay in the summer if you have a beach property.

You can also decide whether to accept same day requests and at what time of the day to shut them off – so you don't get a booking in the middle of the night for a person who wants to check-in immediately. Again, you need to do a cost-benefit analysis. Don't forget; you can play around with this.

When developing your listing, you need to decide on cancellation policies, and how strict about making them. For the three options - Flexible, Medium, and Strict - see <u>Airbnb</u>. You will need to decide how strict you want to be, keeping in mind that if you are very strict, guests might hesitate to book, while if you are flexible, someone might cancel at the last minute, costing you some possible revenue.

A new addition to Airbnb is the guidebook, which allows hosts to provide recommendations to guests about things to do. Consider contributing, as this will make it more likely that Airbnb will feature you in their preferred listings.

The best way to keep your Airbnb at the highest listing efficiency is by getting as many reservations as possible, which means turning on the automatic pricing tool and using the suggested room rates. This means that you are taking Airbnb's advice, which is based on their copious data.

Note: all these tips apply to any kind of listing, whether you are doing it with or without permission from a landlord. However, if you are doing it without permission, make sure not to put any identifying details on your listing, especially images of the outside of the property. You can also ask Airbnb to hide your exact address until after a guest book.

Chapter Summary

The listing is where your property comes to life, so do not be afraid to put your personality into it. Remember, you can always play around with the different sections, so try out different things and see what works for you!

Next Practical Actions to Take

- Preview other listings and take notes on what you like
- Write a few sample titles for your listing and ask friends to weigh in on them

CHAPTER 15: HOW TO MANAGE MULTIPLE LISTINGS ON AIRBNB

Managing multiple listings on Airbnb should only happen after you get the hang of doing one and have built a great reputation. Luckily, Airbnb makes it easy as the hosting section of the platform allows you to move between multiple listings with the tap of the screen.

When you think you are ready, there are great resources for learning more about managing multiple listings, such as this website and podcast.

Things to consider when managing multiple listings include:

- Hiring a cleaning service

- Using a property management company OR: using property management systems, such as YourPorter App.

  o As you select one, be mindful of how much they are charging and avoid getting hit with high fees

  o Read third party reviews before committing to one! Or ask in a host forum.

- Automating your guest messages – remember, if your reply rate goes down, your ranking goes down as well.

- Automating check-in / check-out process

- Developing your market niche. While you might want to attract all guests, it is better to niche down and make your properties known for something special.

Chapter Summary

Multiple listings are the way to earn the most from your Airbnb experience, but you also have to be smart about how you do it. Luckily a whole host of industries have produced technology to help you do it as painlessly as possible – for a price. Be smart when handing over your cash to property managers, in person or digital.

Next Practical Actions to Take

- Research cleaning services
- Research property management companies or apps
- Talk to experienced hosts on the Airbnb forum
- Keep honing your niche.

CHAPTER 16: A PICTURE TELLS A THOUSAND WORDS

As we have discussed, photography is essential to create a successful listing. When planning out your images, you need to make sure to use light properly – if you are inexperienced, check out this short tutorial. Shoot during the day, turn on all the lights and open all the windows, for starters.

You also need to make sure to capture a true representation of the space, so guests can feel what the place is really like. For this reason, corner shots are particularly important, while wall shots make the space look smaller. If you have a stunning view, consider panoramic shots – otherwise, avoid them as they look amateurish. There is no need to use any models in your photography, as most listings do not contain people, allowing guests to envision themselves in the space.

In terms of aspect ratios and resolutions keep a 3:2 ratio to avoid distortion and make sure to have a minimum resolution of 1024 x 683px, according to this blogger.

Highlight your unique amenity and furniture with your images, as this blogger suggests. Local imagery, especially if you are accessible to the site, can make guests feel like you will provide a true, authentic experience.

Finally, you might want to take a personal image and attach it, to make the guest feel like they know who will be welcoming them.

Photography Tricks

People love pets. This is a secret that has helped people on dating apps as well as on Airbnb: put a cute pet in your photo, and people are more likely to stop and notice it. Of course, only do this if you have a pet-friendly listing!

The Advantages of Professional Photography

If you cannot reliably do your own photoshoot, take advantage of the fact that Airbnb will send a professional photographer to your home. Since Airbnb wants its hosts to be as successful as possible – since their income depends upon it – they are eager to connect hosts with professional photographers. Doing so, pays off: according to Airbnb, listings with professional photos have a 40 percent increase in earnings, 24 percent more bookings and a 26 percent higher nightly rate, compared to other comparable hosts in their area. Even better, because the pictures are certified, prospective guests know they are actual photos of your listing and not some fake picture you downloaded from a stock photo site. In terms of arranging payment, you do not even have to lay out any money: Airbnb will deduct the cost from future bookings. They predict that within three bookings, the photos will be paid for, depending on your actual listing.

Chapter Summary

Put your best foot forward with good photography, with plenty of light, corner shots and high resolution. Highlight your unique amenities and local sites, and when in doubt, consider hiring a professional! It'll be worth it.

Next Practical Actions to Take

- Clean up your space for the shoot
- Watch some tutorials on photography tips if needed
- Take some practice shots and ask a friend's opinion
- Consider booking a professional

CHAPTER 17: THE PRICE IS RIGHT

A lot of potential hosts are confused about pricing. However, pricing an Airbnb property is easier than you think. You can simply start by studying what the competition does for pricing, making sure to note that pricing is dependent on different types of property, as well as the time of year. Finding the perfect pricing strategy will depend on your goals and demographics, whether you want to be an elite property that books less often at a higher rate or a popular property that is more affordable. This is why targeting demographic groups is so important because you cannot mismatch the price and the demographic.

First, you need to set your base price – we recommend you pick a price that uses the psychology of "significant digit pricing," which means charging $59 instead of $60, or $199 instead of $200 as the digit nine makes people round down to $50 or $100. Airbnb will provide suggestions, and you can also use AirDNA to get more ideas. Then you need to think about determining base prices for new listings, which means likely lowering the price below what you want to achieve, in order to get higher reviews at first – try at least 10% to start. Then you can determine base prices for older listings, once you get the reviews coming in.

Finally, in order to adjust the price to fit demand, you can rely on the Airbnb price calculator, setting max and a min price, which can always be modified or shut off for specific days and weeks, in case you disagree with their suggestion.

Chapter Summary

Pricing is an art, but luckily you can constantly tweak it, using Airbnb's many tools as well as third party services.

Next Practical Actions to Take

- Study your competition's pricing

- Try out AirDNA

- Make sure you know how much you need to earn from your property and then calculate if it is feasible based on your base price. Remember Airbnb takes a small percentage from you!

CHAPTER 18: BEWARE THE TAXMAN

One of the major responsibilities of an Airbnb host is to pay taxes. For the United States-based hosts, Airbnb only sends Form **1099**-K if you earn over $20,000 and have at least 200 or more reservations in the previous year.

Because tax laws vary so widely in different countries, it is impossible to provide a comprehensive guide. Here are a few things to keep in mind as you prepare yourself:

- Keep a list of all your expenses for possible write-offs, including supplies, utilities, improvements, etc. If you rent a percentage of your property (i.e., a room in your house), you may be able to write off that percentage of expenses, including things like your media subscriptions and your property taxes.

- Check out <u>Airbnb's</u> recommendations for various hosting scenarios.

- When in doubt, use an accountant!

Chapter Summary

Nothing is certain in life but death and taxes, so make sure to keep yourself covered by keeping good records of your expenses. Use Airbnb's resources to get more info, and if you have any questions, get professional help.

Next Practical Actions to Take

- What will be your system for tracking your expenses?
- Inform yourself about your local tax obligations.

CHAPTER 19: LISTING IN A TOURIST DESTINATION AND MANAGING VACATION HOMES

This chapter will highlight the benefits and drawbacks of finding properties for Airbnb in hot tourist destinations and what you can do with them. It will also discuss how to manage any vacation properties.

Listing in Hot Destinations

The obvious advantage of doing Airbnb in a hot tourist destination is a simple fact that your occupancy will never be an issue. There will be a steady stream of guests, and if you do have an off-season, it will be way less noticeable than in less popular places. On the downside, you will have to work harder to get the property to begin with, competing heavily if you want to buy a place and negotiating carefully with your landlord if you want to use arbitrage to rent out your rental (because remember, you can more easily be replaced as a tenant if the landlord does not like the terms of your proposal).

Other drawbacks to consider when deciding to open an Airbnb in a touristy location is the potential for the city to institute a crackdown on short term rentals. As a result of negative publicity, stemming from angry residence, Airbnb has faced major blowback in cities such as Barcelona, New York, and San Francisco, as this article discusses. People are angry about rising rents and declining inventory, as more people decide to rent their properties short term rather than the long term. Others are angry about residential neighborhoods turning into party zones and beautiful or sacred spaces being overrun with a new influx of experience seeking tourists. Hotels might be mad about lower occupancy rates. So, make sure to do your due diligence when going into one of these areas, so that you do not risk making a major decision and then find out it was a mistake.

Managing Your Vacation Property

In the case of setting up an Airbnb in a hot location, you should very seriously consider enlisting a property manager to take care of it or, at the very least, should talk to one to get an idea of what you are in for. Is your destination popular with drunk spring break kids? Make a very strict policy on damage and raise the security deposit to avoid unpleasant surprises. Is your destination meant for families? Consider adding family-friendly features like a high chair, a portable crib, or childproof rooms. Is it a romantic getaway kind of place? Choose your décor accordingly.

You also should find out what the market demands are and what kinds of amenities are most desirable in these locations, as that will help your ability to command top dollar. For instance, in the mountain community of Boone North Carolina, Airbnb recommends a property with a hot tub, because they have data suggesting such amenity is highly desirable. So, pay attention to these clues in your area and try to match the desired amenities, to enjoy the extra boost in the listing.

Chapter Summary

Vacation rentals are their own challenge, especially with the increased scrutiny faced by Airbnb in many major cities today. So be careful and be smart, making sure to read up on how your proposed location is responding to Airbnb. Once you take care of that, be ready to have to work harder to get your property. Then, you will have to be extra attentive about your market demographics, which can really give you a boost in bookings. Some extra house rules and a higher security deposit will help too. Finally, a property management company is highly recommended in these situations.

Next Practical Actions to Take

- Is your desired location in the crosshairs for restrictive anti-Airbnb laws? Do your due diligence and do not get caught unawares.

- Talk to a local property manager just to do some fact-finding or consider hiring them.

- Study the expected amenities in your area in order to position yourself best on the site.

CHAPTER 20: HOW TO PROMOTE YOUR AIRBNB LISTING

Airbnb will passively promote your listing on their site, but you can only move up in the search results by improving your standing on the site – by getting more reviews and higher scores, and by being a responsive host. While you should do those things, you should also be working on your own to boost your visibility. Here are a few ideas.

Building Your Email Mailing list

Airbnb wants you to communicate on their platform, and so they make it difficult to exchange contact information, for example, they will delete anything they think is a phone number or an email from the chats. However, when a guest stays with you, you can do things the "old fashioned" way – ask for their email via a guest book left in the home. By collecting guest messages, you can send out blasts with promotional offers, every so often. There are also third-party apps that will message guests for you. The email mailing list is the best way to create and grow your community, because it reminds people of you on a periodic basis, allowing them to have you fresh in their mind for their next trip or when a friend is traveling to your area. , Also, you can use your mailing list to announce when you acquire new properties and help drive up bookings in a property that does not have many reviews. Since these people are repeat customers, you know they will give you good reviews when they come back – a nice bonus!

As you build your mailing list, you can also be savvy and use it to build a following by offering useful details to the subscribers, like tourism info on your town. An advanced hosting tip is that you can write a small eBook about your town, with insider deals, and then offer it for free to anyone who signs up on your mailing list. Think topics like San Francisco on $40 a day, or The London No Tourist Ever Sees.

If you do not want to make a mailing list, consider an Instagram or Facebook account for your listing, and then posting cool tips and images on a regular basis.

Other Promotional Ideas

Once you have a mailing list, the following ideas become even more potent. This website gives the following suggestions for promoting Airbnb listings:

1. Create a Story to Promote Your Airbnb Listing on Social Media: this is a good way to leverage your current network to expand your reach. If your listing is catered to businesspeople, try using LinkedIn. If you are looking for younger guests, try Instagram and use creative hashtags and even a little video to get more views. If you are looking for older guests and families, Facebook might be the right platform. Just make sure to have great visuals to go with it.

2. Work with a Journalist or Lifestyle. Blogger: Freelance writers always need a story, so look at the publications you like and contact the writers to see if they are interested. To do this, you need a cool angle about your property, whether it just looks really fashionable, or you have a good personal perspective to share. Do not get discouraged if it takes a while to hear back from them and try multiple journalists.

3. Create a Unique URL to Promote Your Airbnb Listing: this means picking a more memorable name for your listing that connects to your Airbnb page, which you can use to direct guests to it more quickly. Think creatively: "PrincetonPurpleHouse" will be more likely to stick in someone's mind than just the generic Airbnb page.

4. Join Vacation Rental Forums: this is an indirect way of building your referrals by networking with hosts. If you are a good community member, it will be more likely that other hosts will send you some business if they know of someone going to your area.

5. Get Listed with Tourism Websites in Your Area: this is the best way to get free advertising outside of Airbnb, as local tourism boards are eager to help increase occupancy in their town.

6. Create Business Cards and Flyers: you can leave these in hotspots around town, like cafes, the library and campuses. Even local hospitals might have boards for advertising. Often referrals will come from locals who are having guests in town but cannot fit them in their own property, so don't be afraid to post your ads in places where locals go. If you post in tourist spots, you will find people who already found their accommodations!

7. Create Special Offers for Your Guests: everyone loves a deal, so take advantage of buyer psychology and offer a discount. Note, Airbnb will sometimes give you the option to list a small discount for an unbooked day or two, usually only a few days in advance. Then they will advertise for you to anyone searching in your area for those days. However, this option appears randomly and is out of your control if it does not appear, so do not count on it.

8. Submit Photos of Your Property to Design Blogs: if your place is gorgeous and unique, and you have nice professional photography, this is a great option. If not, forget it!

Chapter Summary

Build a mailing list and a social media following, and you will have lots of opportunities to increase your visibility and your occupancy rates. Whether your place is fancy or just normal, there are lots of opportunities to market, digitally and with traditional methods. Eventually, when your listing starts rising in popularity, you will appear at the top of the Airbnb search, but before that happens – and in order to make that happen sooner – try out these techniques and see what you can achieve. The best part of this is – most of these advertising options are free or very low cost, so they are easy to try out.

Next Practical Actions to Take

Decide which of the suggestions are most attractive to you, and then take the steps to see if they are able. Try:

- contacting your local tourism board,
- googling some lifestyle bloggers,
- posting to social media
- creating a unique IRL
- joining a vacation host forum

CHAPTER 21: HOW TO MANAGE GUESTS

Guest relations are the heart of the Airbnb experience. This chapter will talk all about the best way to manage your guest relations and why this is so important. It will address issues like guest communication, the rule book, and how to stop problems before they start. It will also have suggestions for check-in and check-out, and finally, it will have a section on problem guests: what to do in the event of damage or misuse of the property, additional guests being brought in without permission, and payment issues.

Guest Communication

Guest communication starts from the moment of inquiry or booking. A guest will be required to send you a little message. Sometimes they will tell you something about themselves and why they are coming, other messages will be much briefer. You should reply to this message right away and set a positive tone for their stay. (Note: you can save commonly used messages in the Airbnb app and simply send it out with a tap or two – but an individual touch is nice, if you have the time. There are also apps that you can sync with your Airbnb to do this for you automatically.) For example, one host we interviewed who has children in his home, which is above the rental property, sends out a greeting message letting people know that they might hear the kids' footsteps in the morning and evening. This helps set expectations for noise and, if the person is totally against this, allows them to cancel – which helps avoid getting grumpy guests who leave bad reviews.

Then a second message should be sent as their check-in day nears. You can provide additional information about check-in or leave this information in the "check-in guidelines" Airbnb provides for you to fill out. You can plan to meet them if you want to be a more hand-on the host. You can also inquire about their check-in time, even if you do not plan to meet them, so you can make sure the property is ready in terms of cleaning.

A third message should be sent a little after checking in – soon after, if you did not meet them, and perhaps the next day, if you did meet them. This message should ask them if they need anything and make sure they are having a comfortable stay. Depending on the length of the stay, you could send a fourth message with check out instructions, an additional offer for help, and a thank you. (And if you need to know their check out time, you can politely ask.) Finally, goodbye and thank you message should get sent after they check out. This is when you can request that they leave you a review and tell them you would be happy to host them again.

This kind of healthy, regular communication will allow guests to feel cared for – but not micromanaged. It will allow for some nice exchange of pleasantries and make sure that the guest sees you as someone they can address any issues with – so that they do not wait until the review and then complain about something you never saw coming!

Check-in and Check out

There are many ways to deal with the check-in and check-out process, that will depend on your availability, the specificities of your property and your guest's needs. Having a plan to accommodate late check-ins (and early check-outs) is crucial, as many guests need it – and sometimes things come up, such as a delayed flight, that makes it imperative that a guest can come and go as they need. To be realistic, you do not want to have to be on call at 4 in the morning! The easiest way to deal with this is to install a lock box or a smart lock that allows a guest to check-in just using a code you provide or their smartphone. These are easy to install and well worth the investment. Another low-tech possibility is to have an agreed hiding spot for the key (if you live in a safe area). If you live in an urban area, you might ask a trusted store owner of a 24-hour shop to hold your key for you.

Then there is the other issue, of a guest requesting to check in early or check out late. This is up to you and depends on your other bookings and your cleaning schedule. To be a nice host, it is always good to try to let people check-in and out when best suits them. This gives them a welcoming feeling. Now if you have back to back late check-outs and early check-ins, you might not have time for cleaning, so try to compromise with them if possible. Then, you have to either make yourself available to clean in a very small window or having your cleaning service be prepared to come. The best way to handle this is to schedule the cleaning at 12:30 pm every day, which allows for both a late checkout and early check-in, unless the property is enormous and requires hours of cleaning, in which case you might not want to allow back to back check-ins anyway!

Guest Problems

There is no doubt if you host long enough, you will run into issues, but the hosts we interviewed only discussed minor issues. Most people are respectful of rules, so take time to plan out your rule book – you can even print out a copy and leave it laminated on a table in your place, perhaps next to welcoming brochures about local activities and restaurants.

If a guest damages your property, Airbnb has a simple procedure to deal with it. You have to report it promptly, and make sure to take photographs. Then you can address the issue with the guest directly and ask for a reimbursement. If they say no, Airbnb will escalate it and ask for more evidence from both sides: for example if they stain your sheets, which is a very common occurrence, you have to provide receipts showing how much they cost or how much it would be to replace them. During this time, you have customer support in contact with you constantly.

If there is a misuse of your property, you can first try to deal with the guest directly, either through messages or in person. If it happens and you find out about it after, you can simply leave a bad review. If the guest gets enough bad reviews, they will not be able to use the platform. If the misuse involves sneaking in other guests in order to pay extra fees, you have to decide if it is worth it to do something. (The best way to find out if this is happening is by using a video camera security door-bell.) If it is a question of $10 extra that they owe you, it might not be worth the trouble. You can mention it to them, and people will often apologize and offer to pay if they are caught. You can also leave them a bad review and not recommend them, but it is usually better to talk first; it could be a genuine mistake on their part. If it is a lot of money that they owe you, you can get Airbnb involved in a dispute. Again, always remember to strike a balance because you do want good reviews, so do not go overboard.

Finally, regarding dealing with payment issues, the great news is that you do not have to! One of the reasons why hosts pay Airbnb a percentage is because Airbnb takes care of that for you. The guest pro-vides the credit card, and if there are any issues with it, the host is noti-fied before the stay. If the card fails, you have the option to cancel the booking with no penalty.

Chapter Summary

Make sure to be in touch with your guests. If everything is smooth, three to four messages per visit should be enough. A thorough rulebook will prevent problems, and when problems do occur, if they are serious, Airbnb will help you out. If they are minor, consider whether it is worth it, in the end, to really be aggressive about getting what you want with one single guest. Remember, you do want good reviews, so it might be best to play nice while they are there. After you leave, you can always leave them a bad review, and you can always refuse to host them in the future if it really did not work out. There will be more guests!

Next Practical Actions to Take

- If you already have an account on Airbnb, go ahead and write out four standard messages to use with guests at the different stages of their visit. You can label and save them and edit them for future occasions.

- Think about your late check-in / early check out and how you will handle it. Now is a great time to investigate electronic locks or other possible low-tech solutions.

- What is your policy for early check-in and late checkout? How will you adapt to cleaning?

- Start thinking about your rule book and how you will use it to set expectations (see chapter 34 for more information and details).

- Review Airbnb policies for damage and guest complaints, including what to do in the event of damage. This will help keep you calm when you actually need to do something about it.

CHAPTER 22: HOW TO GET REVIEWS

This chapter will talk specifically about everything you will need to do to make sure you get consistent five-star reviews every time, as well as how to deal with bad reviews when they inevitably happen.

First off, before we talk about getting *good* reviews, let's talk about getting *any* reviews. The best way to get a large number of reviews, which will make your property seem attractive, is by starting off with a lower price to attract more bookings. A lower price will also make people feel like they got a good deal and may lead to higher-quality reviews. The next thing to do to make sure you get reviews is to ask for them – you can leave a nicely written note in the Airbnb asking your guests to leave their feedback, and telling them to please let you know if there is anything that you can do to make their stay better. You could say something like, "Your five-star review means so much to us, please let us know if there is anything, we can do to be sure to earn it," or some other words that capture your personality. This will help make sure that they can let you know of any problems and correct them before it is too late.

Being punctual with leaving your own reviews for guests will also help, as they will be notified that you reviewed them and be more inspired to write one for you while the memory is still fresh in their mind.

Meeting your guests at check-in and following up with them during their stay is another great way to encourage positive reviews, because you establish a personal connection with them, which tends to inspire empathy and higher review scores.

Getting a bad review is a totally normal part of the process. There will be inevitable guests who are just grumpy, and you will have no idea until they left the review. There are other guests who think that five stars are only for 100% perfection. First off, if you get an occasional bad review once you have a lot of reviews, you should not think about it and worry at all. If the vast majority are good, future guests know that some people can be grumpy and rude. If you get an aggressive review, you can post a reply in which you act professional and restrained (never passive-aggressive or aggressive), and you apologize for whatever grievance they are posting about. The last thing you want is to come off as a jerk, even if they seem totally out of line. If there is a specific problem, you might say that you are fixing in. If the review is totally out of line, you can write to customer service and see about it being deleted.

Pro tip: sometimes you have a guest and you just have a bad feeling about how their review is going to be. After fourteen days, their review will be public no matter what, but you can avoid reviewing them until the last possible moment so that their bad review will not be posted to your profile for those two weeks. Then, in the meantime, you will have other guests leaving good reviews, which you can make visible immediately by reviewing them in turn. This is important because the most recent review is the one that will appear right under your listing and will be the one that new guests will see first.

Pro tip number 2: Airbnb has a great feature where guests can select pre-determined criticisms and compliments for you and when they start to form a pattern, it can be valuable information for you as you respond to your reviews. Are you regularly getting praised or critiqued for cleaning? How about for your "thoughtful touches"? Do you have enough towels available? Spend some time reviewing these issues and look out for trends. If you address them, your reviews are sure to improve as well.

Chapter Summary

Keep your prices down, get your bookings up and your reviews will start to flood in. Ask your guests to review you and review them promptly. Make sure to be a great host and offer to correct any problems if they come up. If you get a bad review, do not sweat it too much – they happen! Reply professionally and calmly, and just concentrate on doing it better next time.

Next Practical Actions to Take

- Questions to ask yourself: what made me give a five-star review when I was hosting? If you ever gave a lower review, why?

- Are guests complaining about something regularly in your property? What can you do to fix that issue, so it does not come up again?

CHAPTER 23: AUTOMATION IS KING

Today everything is automated, or at least it can be. So, consider taking advantage of all the tools out there to improve your hosting experience, especially when scaling up.

To automate check-in, you can do one of three things, according to this blog: use a lockbox, use a building concierge or hire someone. Another way to automate is by using Airbnb management software. The advantages, according to this blog are flawless communication with guests, increased reviews, ease of managing multiple properties, increased team efficiency, and a possibly higher ranking on the Airbnb page. The cons are that the software all has a cost and there could be a failure of the technology that could create a mess with your guest. Most management software also allows for automatic replies and messages.

See the security and technology chapters for more information on how automation can make things easier and safer for your Airbnb.

Chapter Summary

- Automation is every host's friend, so do your homework and see how you can make your hosting experience seamless. With a little research and a small investment, you can automate your Airbnb in order to make it as efficient as possible. Just make sure to have a backup plan if something fails!

Next Practical Actions to Take

- Consider automating your check-in, by investigating lockboxes

- Compare software options here.

- What is your back up plan if your software fails? How will you communicate with guests and vice versa?

CHAPTER 24: REAL ESTATE AND AIRBNB

Real estate markets are in constant flux, so the best way to be sure you are making a smart real estate investment is to use trusted online tools for gauging those markets in real-time. One such tool is available at mashvisor.com. Others include Investopedia, which uses AirDNA to list the top US cities for profitable hosting, based on the difference between potential earnings and average mortgage costs, as:

1. Palm Springs, CA
2. Lahaina, HI
3. Davenport FL
4. Bend, OR
5. Nashville, TN

Another website argues that Miami and San Diego are the most profitable cities for hosts, based on the tool Beyond Pricing.

Don't forget there are other things to consider beyond absolute profit: not all properties are equally profitable in different markets. Some places might be better to rent a room, whereas in other places only full houses do well. If rents or mortgages are higher, then your costs will go up, so that is another thing to keep in mind.

Chapter Summary

Real estate markets are notoriously unstable, so it's a lucky thing there are so many sites and tools that are geared to helping Airbnb hosts figure out where to try their luck. Many of them are subscription-based, so do your research before committing – and cross-check multiple services.

Next Practical Actions to Take

- Look at the different tools and read reviews of them before committing to a subscription.

- Hopefully you have a few potential cities in mind, so research how they compare using one of the tools or sites listed above.

CHAPTER 25: SCALING UP

Congratulations! If you are reading for this chapter, it means your first property is going well. However, even if you have a high-end listing, there are only 365 days per year, so there is a limit to how much you can make. This chapter will talk all about how to scale up your Airbnb business to six-figures a year and the strategy behind doing so.

Multiple Listings

In order to make $100,000 per year, you only have to make $273 per day, at 100% occupancy. The fastest way to get there is through multiple listings. See chapter fifteen for more on how to manage multiple listings.

A few things to think about: what is your niche and how can you expand your niche by acquiring multiple properties strategically? As you build your client base, people will want to come to you for more of what they originally liked. So, if you have multiple ski cabins, that will allow them to have options if you are booked at once.

There are advantages to diversifying as well, for example, getting beach properties across the world, but then you will have to handle a lot of other issues, like getting different property managers and learning about different local laws.

A great way to have multiple listings is by buying a multi-unit property, such as a duplex or a house with an in-law or back yard cabin. That way you can rent to large or small groups, and you can have everything in a single geographical location. You can also share expenses, such as internet and TV services, insurance, etc., and provide shared amenities, such as patio furniture for all to share.

Developing a business mindset

Having one Airbnb listing is a side job while scaling up means having a proper business and, therefore, developing a business mindset. This means:

- Not taking anything personally

- Striving to always make the customer happy

- Realizing that marketing is an on-going effort

- Relying on trusted help

- Knowing how to spend money to make money (you can be frugal without being cheap)

- Keeping good relationships with any landlords and neighbors

- Keeping abreast of trends affecting Airbnb locally and internationally

- Keeping track of profitability and reassessing whether a property is a good investment on a regular basis. When it is time to sell, sell, without getting too sentimental about the property.

Coming up with a business plan

As with all endeavors in life, if you fail to plan, you plan to fail. A business plan is a key part of scaling a business. This means you need to carefully do the math **to compare numbers of property versus the amount of profit you expect to make. If you do not have experience doing this, here are some steps you should take, according to this blog:**

Step 1. Analyze the local market: AirDNA and other sites are great for this. Be sure to think about cost versus profitability.

Step 2. Identify unique selling points about your Airbnb business (i.e., what is your niche?)

Step 3. Identify the marketing strategies that you will use (see chapter 20)

Step 4. Decide on the Airbnb management structure that you will use, including any automation or management company (see chapter 23)

Step 5. Formulate your operations plan (do you need any employees and how much will they cost?)

Step 6. Write a comprehensive financial plan. According to Mashvisor, this needs to include:

- How are you going to finance the investment property? This is important in order to estimate cash flow and the net operating income.

- What is your cash flow for the next year?

- Does a growth analysis to predict your five-year plan?

- Keep your long-term financial goals in mind.

Step 7. Get all your documentation in order (if you need to find investors or apply for a mortgage this will be crucial sooner rather than later; it will also be needed for your taxes.)

Building a team

You might want to go it alone, but when you scale, that becomes impossible – and that means you are doing something right. A good team includes a co-host (unless you want to automate), a cleaning staff (that can come at a moment's notice), and emergency contacts that can handle everything from lockouts to accidents. This might simply mean hiring property managers, as they usually handle every aspect listed above. Do not forget to factor in these costs when doing your business plan.

Automating

As discussed in chapter 23, automation is key to a successful Airbnb endeavor, allowing you to be working *on* the business not in the business.

Chapter Summary

If you're ready to scale, it means that your six-figure income is closer than you think. When it is time to scale, you have to repeat all the processes you went through when you started, in terms of picking a property, getting it set up and managing it. But luckily, now you are already an expert. Do not cut any corners, though, and make sure you have a solid plan, including concrete financial planning.

Next Practical Actions to Take

- What are you waiting for? Now is the time to write a financial plan. If you have a trusted financial adviser, ask them for help. Otherwise, there are lots of online courses for small businesses that can help you. Many Airbnb hosts offer their own "experience" seminars to teach how to do this – you could even do one in the future.

CHAPTER 26: TIMESCALES FROM BEGINNING TO END

Here is your checklist of everything that needs to be done to get yourself started on Airbnb from nothing.

Pre-Planning

- Stay in other people's Airbnb's to build your profile and learn about what you like

- Decide whether you will be renting or buying

- Find your desired area

- Research it is using Airbnb and AirDNA

- Project how much you can earn and how much it costs to rent or buy

- Make your financial plan to calculate how soon you will be making money and to know your budget for the property, as well as marketing, furnishing, etc.

- Identify the desired property

- Find out any local laws about Airbnb, permits, restrictions, taxes, etc.

- Prepare to speak with the landlord / find a realtor to help you purchase

- Negotiate the terms of the rental/purchase

- Getting ready to rent

- Decide who is your ideal guest

- What special features will you have to cater to them?

- Plan your design, furnishing and gadgets with them in mind

- Enlist design help or shop for your property

- Write your listing, your guest rules, and your guidebook

- Decide your policies such as discounts, cancellation, accepting kids, etc.

- Photograph your listing

- Decide on an initial price for the listing

- Stay in your property overnight to experience it as a guest would

- Make your operations plan, including any co-hosts, cleaning services, etc.

- Publish your listing

- Ask friends and family to put the property on their Wishlist

- Market your listing, thinking about your demographic targets

Renting

- Reply to guest inquiries promptly

- Make sure your guests have an excellent stay

- Don't forget to ask for reviews

- Update your prices as necessary, after obtaining superhost status

- Check your reviews regularly to identify any problems

- Stay at your property regularly to make sure it stays high quality

- Prepare for any low season

- Make sure to refresh the décor and linens as they age

- Consider automation, testing out different software before you scale

- Consider property management or a co-host

- Regularly advertise to your mailing list and social media channels

Scaling

- Once your property is stable, and you are a superhost, it's time to scale

- Craft a business plan with five year and long-term goals.

- Identify additional properties, keeping in mind how you want to grow your niche.

- Identify potential investors and approach them.

- Make sure your automation processes are set

- Have a good team in place

- Take the plunge and get your next property

- Advertise to your mailing list and social media channels, considering the possibility of offering deals.

- Repeat according to your goals and plans!

CHAPTER 27: QUICK SECRETS FOR CASHING IN ON AIRBNB, PLUS A COUPLE OF ADVANCED SECRETS

Want a quick win on Airbnb? Try these tricks:

Attract guests who are going on random vacations by lowering your weekend prices for any weekend that is unbooked a few days in advance.

Is there a big festival or event in your area? Try cashing in by informing yourself of what is going on and raising your prices. You could even get the organizers to list you as a possible place to stay.

Do you have a one-bedroom apartment? This can be a major advantage, as sometimes less is more. Check out these tips for making a small space popular!

Advanced Secrets

Need discounted furniture? Try local furniture outlets, or better yet, estate sales to pick up unique and discounted pieces. If you live in a student area, try scooping up furniture in May and June when they move out of their student housing for the summer.

Discounted linens are easier to find than ever, either online from Amazon.com or overstock.com or in overstock stores like Tuesday Morning.

Are you thinking about hiring staff and engaging with property managers? Consider using AirDNA in order to evaluate them, or look on rented.com.

Chapter Summary

If you are smart enough to look around, there are lots of quick tips to making your Airbnb successful, in terms of scoring last-minute bookings or finding cheap cool furnishings!

Next Practical Actions to Take

- Make a list of how you plan to cash in. Are there local festivals you can take advantage of? Random vacations?

- Think about your plan for finding discounted furniture and linens.

- Are you hiring staff? What is your plan for finding the best people?

CHAPTER 28: SLOW SEASON

Most locations world-wide have a slow season, whether it is in the winter for a beach property or those dreary weeks after New Year's Eve when fewer people travel, even to top destinations like New York City and London. The slow season could also refer to a regular part of the week: if you live in a business hub, you might be busier during weekdays, and if you live in a tourist spot, expect to be busier on the weekends.

Luckily, a slow season does not have to mean that your income must dry up or that your business model goes out the window. This chapter will dive specifically into the slow season - what to do when there is one and what you can do about it.

Here are a few ideas on how to combat the slow season and continue to make good profits. According to one blogger, the first thing to do is a have a strict financial plan to guide you through the year, making sure you know what are your permanent expenses (you have a mortgage or rent to pay, whether or not you have guests, same goes with amenities like Netflix) and what are your contingent expenses (you only have to pay for breakfast and cleaning supplies if you have guests). Once you have this information spelled out, you can figure out how much you can afford to cut your price in the off season. This blogger cites a statistic that recommends as much as a forty percent cut in listing price in order to keep occupancy up.

A second tip is to allow instant booking: this allows guests who meet your requirements to book automatically, avoiding any wasted time. This encourages guests to go ahead and book your place over another place where they might have to make an inquiry first. It has an added bonus that it makes your listing appear higher in search placements (and, along with that, it will help you to reach superhost status faster if you get more bookings as a result). There are some drawbacks because you often get guests who are in a rush. This could mean that they do not fully read about your listing and then are upset when something does not meet their standards or expectations. It could mean they do not follow house rules. It also can mean that you get the last-minute guest you were not prepared for. (The best way to find a compromise around this issue is to use the setting that gives a "cut off" time for instant bookings, which means people might not be allowed to instant book within a certain window. You can choose same-day instant bookings and set your cut off time – this will avoid getting an instant booking in the middle of the night – or you can say they can take only instant book one or more days in advance. This, of course, lowers the number of bookings, but might just save your sanity.) Finally, this blogger recommends being more flexible about house rules – consider allowing pets during the off-season (with clear policies about what happens if there is damage, etc.) or even relaxing your rule about no parties (again with clear policies and discussions with the guest).

There are also more advanced techniques, such as figuring out who your ideal off-season guest is, based on past off seasons if you had any, and then directly marketing to them. You can send messages to past off-season guests with special offers if they book again. Another great idea from one blogger is to contact the organizers of events and festivals, asking them to list your place as possible accommodation for their guests – organizers always provide listings, usually using hotels, but why not try? Consider giving a special rate for people in town for that event.

Another possibility is to offer a "friends and family" Airbnb Discount, according to this blogger. There is an automated service called Smartbnb that will automatically send out a customizable message to your guests a week after they check out that will inform them that they are eligible for an extra X% discount – and so are their friends and family, if they mention the guest by name during the low peak season.

Another advanced strategy for dealing with the slow season is not to have one! What do we mean by that? Well, if you are smart enough to own properties in multiple areas, you might move between them so that you occupy the property that is currently in an off season and rent the one that is in the high season. Perhaps you spend the winter at the beach and free up your mountain cabin in the ski season, and spend the summer in your mountain cabin, leaving the beach house free.

Finally, ask yourself if your listing is up to the highest standards. Remember, it is possible to earn money in the off season, but you will be competing for fewer tourism dollars. So, make sure to put your best foot forward. Now is the time to improve your photography, if necessary, and polish up your profile if it is not already perfect.

Chapter Summary

This chapter gave you lots of ideas to get prepared for the slow season if you are in an area that has one. This means making sure you have a good business model, that you consider relaxing some of your requirements, that you step up your marketing efforts and that you leverage your past guests by offering them future discounts.

Next Practical Actions to Take

- Do you have a slow season in your proposed area? Do some research to make sure you are aware of what that season might be and how much tourism declines in that period.

- Do you have a business plan? How much do you need to make per month, based on fixed expenses? How much can you afford to cut during the off season?

- What rules can you relax for the off season, if any? Are you willing to allow pets? Parties? Can you turn on instant booking?

- What events, if any, take place during your slow season? Lots of towns will organize events in order to try to improve tourism in a slow season. Make a list and plan to contact organizers to see if they will promote your listing and ask what kind of discount you should offer in exchange.

- Check out Smartbnb and see about automating messages to get in touch with past guests to offer low season friends and family discounts.

- Consider buying properties with different off-seasons and plan to move between them to maximize earnings, if your lifestyle allows it.

- Finally, is your listing being up to the highest standards? Consider it might be time to improve your photography or to try to polish up your profile if it is not already perfect!

CHAPTER 29: WHAT YOU MIGHT NOT HAVE CONSIDERED

This chapter will focus on things you might not have considered, to give you better insight into the Airbnb experience:

Leveraging AirDNA data: this is a no-brainer, and if you are not doing it, you are losing out on a major source of potential revenue.

Accepting children/infants: this is a branding question every host must answer. Is your listing child-friendly? Airbnb lets you select this as an option, and if you want to accept kids, make sure your place is childproof, that your furniture is durable and easy to clean (no white carpets!), and that you have a sufficient security deposit to cover potential losses. If you want to accept kids, go all the way and provide portable cribs, high chairs, toys, etc., and make your images reflect that. If you want to discourage kids, you should be clear about that as well, emphasizing potential hazards like steep stairs, or lots of breakables. It is all part of your demographic niching, so think this one through.

Co-hosting: do you want to use a co-host and, if so, how much are they getting paid? Are they a partner or an assistant? Co-hosts are a great option to help you manage the property, and Airbnb has enabled this feature on its site, to allow multiple people access to one account. You can delegate tasks like messaging and replying to inquiries if you want to avoid using automated services. Just remember to have your agreement in writing, so there are no issues

Property management: this is a huge decision and should be based on how much time you have and how much you are willing to spend. We recommend not using one at first so that you really get to know your property and the hosting experience, which will give you the expertise to be able to safely outsource the work without losing out on valuable revenue.

Chapter Summary

Airbnb is a complex system with many different variables that will influence your hosting experience. These details are issuing all hosts should think about when trying to decide what direction to go in.

Next Practical Actions to Take

- Decide whether you will:
  - o use AirDNA
  - o accept children
  - o have a co-host
  - o use a property management company

CHAPTER 30: AIRBNB TERMS

This chapter will focus on general terms people talk about when it comes to Airbnb and what they all mean.

Airbnbing: Depending on whether you are a host or a guest, this might mean renting out your property or staying in an Airbnb.

Airbnb host guarantee: $1,000,000 of coverage in the case of property damage by a guest.

Airbnb host insurance: $1,000,000 of coverage in the case a guest sues because of injury.

Airbnb rental arbitrage: renting a property and then listing it on Airbnb, earning yourself a higher monthly rate than the amount you pay the landlord.

Calendar: This is where you can monitor your bookings and change your availability and pricing.

Cleaning service: a company that will take care of getting your Airbnb ready for guests. May even provide laundry services for a fee.

Co-host: someone you put on your Airbnb account who can monitor the account and reply to guests.

Guidebook: this is something you write to tell guests where to visit. It helps guests have a great experience and helps you get more visibility on the Airbnb site, as they will promote you based on your selections.

Profile: This is where you describe yourself as a host to help guests get to know you.

Property Management Company: a company that will handle every aspect of the Airbnb for a flat fee or a percentage of your earnings.

Property management software: an app that lets you automate your Airbnb, with things like automatic messaging and check-in. Usually costs less than property managers but cannot do things like responding to emergencies.

Response rate: A host's response rate is the percentage of new inquiries and reservation requests he or she responded to (by either accepting or pre-approving or declining) within twenty-four hours in the past thirty days. This is crucial for maintaining a good position on the results page.

Rulebook: This is where you list all your house policies that guests must follow.

Superhost: Superhosts have a response rate of at least 90 percent. They are hosts that have hosted at least ten trips in recent weeks. They do not cancel bookings, and they have earned at least 80 percent five-star ratings.

CHAPTER 31: INSIDER SECRETS: WHAT 99% OF PEOPLE DON'T KNOW WHEN IT COMES TO MAKING MONEY THROUGH AIRBNB

This chapter will focus on the insider secrets of Airbnb, as well as the fundamental key to Airbnb success: how to become and stay a super-host. It also will cover how to effectively use discounts on a daily, weekly and monthly basis

Secrets of Airbnb

Want to know what your guests are experiencing? Try staying in your own property, after all, most people who sell something try it themselves before making it available to the public! One expert <u>host</u> recommends staying in your property at least every few months, in order to best put yourself into the shoes of the most demanding guests. (The off-season can be a great time to do this, to avoid losing high nightly rates). There is more to be a great host than just making the property comfortable and clean from an outsider perspective. Take a shower in your own bathroom! Spend the night in your bed. That way, you will know if you need to unclog a drain or add an extra blanket. How's the reading light in the bedroom? How convenient is it to recharge your devices while staying at the property? Sometimes a small and cheap improvement can make the best impact, but you will not know if you do not see for yourself.

How to Become – and Stay! – A Superhost

What are Superhosts? They are hosts that have a response rate of at least 90 percent. They have completed at least 10 trips (or completed 3 reservations that total at least 100 nights).

They do not cancel bookings hardly ever (they only cancel 1 out of every 100 reservations for a rate of 1% at most), and they maintain a 4.8 overall rating, out of 5. The most obvious way to become a Superhost is by attracting your first ten guests and then making sure you get five-star ratings from them. The quickest way to do this is:

-Have amazing photography (or use a professional provided by Airbnb)

-Set reasonable (low!) pricing (remember, you can change this at any time, so give your early guests a great value to ensure they book and give you high reviews).

-Be careful with setting your availability on your calendar to ensure you will not have to cancel.

-Stay in contact with your guests during their stay. Be there to personally greet them for check-in, send them a "checkup" message during their stay to see if they need anything. Leave notes in your property reminding them to be in touch if they need anything, from toiletries to more fresh towels. Make sure to write to them when they check out, expressing your appreciation.

-Review them promptly to inspire them to review you as well. Remember, you will not be able to see their review of you (and vice versa) until each person writes it, so do not think that you can influence their review with a nice extra review of your own! That would be cheating!

Once you have superhost status, you should continue doing these things in order to keep it. Your status will be reviewed by Airbnb quarterly, and the average is taken over a twelve-month period. This means that when you first get superhost status, you will have to be more attentive to your ratings, as a few four-star reviews could knock you down. Once you have a full year of bookings under your belt, however, a few lower ratings here and there will not meaningfully influence your average.

How to Use Discounts to Your Advantage

Everyone loves a discount, so if you want to have longer-term guests who pay slightly less but give you more reliable income and less work in terms of turn around and clean up, consider using weekly and monthly discounts. Airbnb will select a certain percent discount and recommend it to you, for seven-day stays and an even bigger discount for monthly stays. Their numbers are based on their algorithms so that you can trust them – but you can also decide that if their monthly amount is much lower than what you consistently get per month, to ignore the discount. It depends on how much risk you want to assume how many turnovers you want, and what the trends are in your area.

Chapter Summary

This chapter provided secret tips for Airbnb hosts, like how to make sure your property is great, how to attract people to your listing, how to become a superhost and how to use discounts to your advantage. Remember, being a superhost is just what it sounds like: it means going the extra mile, regularly, for your guests. Getting to become a superhost takes just ten fantastic trips in your first quarter, so if all goes well after three months, you will manage to obtain it. Just remember to set your pricing low at first, have awesome photography and then be genuinely concerned about the happiness of each of your guests. Once you get it, it will become easier to keep it, and you will see your profits increase rather quickly.

Next Practical Actions to Take

- Review your photography. Consider hiring a professional or taking some shots with pets to attract attention.

- Consider employing discounts according to the strategy above.

- Get ready to become a superhost! Review the criteria and make sure you are meeting it as you prepare to host your first guest.

CHAPTER 32: HOW TO STAY SAFE WITH AIRBNB

Airbnb is a community platform and, for the most part, tends to be a safe method of traveling and of earning money. This chapter will focus on the best ways for you to stay safe when using Airbnb. There are two main strategies for doing so: using a guest's profile reviews to screen potential guests and adopting security-focused technology to make your property safer. While nothing in life is one hundred percent guarantee, these commonsense strategies will definitely make a difference in trying to assure your safety.

Profile Reviews

Profile reviews are really the glue that holds the Airbnb community together. They provide an extra assurance that people will not do something dangerous, rude, or inappropriate, because they know that if they do, they risk never being able to use the platform again. Normally reviews are pretty straightforward, but if a guest has a raging party, damages the property or does anything to make the host feel unsafe, their reviews will reflect that. If you see a potential guest with worrisome reviews, feel free to reject the booking. It becomes more difficult if you see a guest who has few or no reviews at all. In that case, you could reject them, but why not start up a little chat with them to see how they respond to some basic questions about their travel. Do not forget, Airbnb also asks guests to verify their identity, so that you can be sure that the person who is booking is not using an assumed name.

Security Technology

If you are hosting a guest within your own house, this becomes more of an issue. There is nothing wrong with installing a substantial lock on your bedroom door and placing security cameras throughout the property. This security <u>website</u> has a list of gadgets meant to help Airbnb hosts stay safe. Check on your local and national laws about your rights and obligations regarding the use of technology.

Common Sense

If you are hosting a guest in a separate property, your biggest concern is the safety of the property itself – which means that the Airbnb host guarantee should be enough to protect you, should any damages be done. The only time when you might need to exercise caution is when checking a guest into the property. If you arrange to give a little "welcome" tour to a guest and for any reason, feel uncomfortable upon meeting them, you might prefer not to enter the property with them alone. In that case, safety first – and feel free to invent an excuse, hand them the keys and leave. (If this becomes a regular issue for you, you might want to hire someone to manage the property for you to avoid potential bad reviews.) However, talking about all these possible precautions should not be a reason to get scared. Even though there is never a full guarantee of anything in life, Airbnb guests tend to be honest people, just looking for a nice local experience.

Chapter Summary

Nothing in life is guaranteed, and you might have some worries around security and your Airbnb. While the Airbnb host guarantees will cover property damage, and the Airbnb reviews do a good job of screening out really bad guests, make sure to take some basic precautions for your personal safety, especially if you will be sharing your own living space with potential guests.

Next Practical Actions to Take

Will you be using security technology in your Airbnb? If so, check into the local and national laws governing surveillance to see if you are allowed to record people in your own home and whether or not you are required to provide them with notice (written or verbal).

Do you give guests a personal tour of your property? If you do, plan what your strategy would be if any guest acted in a way that made you uncomfortable.

CHAPTER 33: EXAMPLES

This chapter will give some practical examples of one of the most important things you need to do to make your Airbnb run smoothly: how to layout things like your rule books for your guests.

Because the rule book is so important for having good hosting experiences, setting expectations and getting good reviews, this is a popular topic in online forums. First, think about what kind of guests you will attract to your home. Is this likely to be a party space, a workspace, a family space, or a romance? Second, think about what environmental concerns you have: are there sensitive neighbors? Issues with parking? Do you share the space and have your own needs for noise and cleanliness? Did your landlord ask you to do or to avoid certain things? One blogger gives the following guidelines to help you prepare to write your rule book, suggesting that you start by asking yourself questions like:

- Are you planning to you allow guests to smoke on your property or any part of it? (Is there a balcony available for smokers?)

- Will you allow pets of any kind? Will pets incur an additional security deposit?

- Do people have to take their shoes off when indoors? (Will you provide indoor sandals or slippers for them?)

- Are there certain activities that are off-limits in certain areas, such as no eating in the bedrooms?

- Can they bring additional overnight guests into the property (if they are not on the reservation?)

- Are there quiet hours?

- Are there shower/water usage limits due to environmental issues?

If it is a shared space, consider…

- Will you allow your guests to use the kitchen? Are there any time limits for this use? What about any food they find in the fridge or cabinets (for instance, only foods in a certain cabinet, like oils and spices, or breakfast foods laid out on a certain shelf on the fridge)?

- Will you allow your guests to use the washer and dryer? If you allow it, are you charging them extra for it? Do you provide detergent and dryer sheets? Is there a limit to how many loads they can do?

- Any time limits on certain activities, like no showers after a certain time?

Keep in mind it is important to strike a balance between being specific in your rules and not seeming too controlling, as that can really put off guests and make them feel unwelcome. As you write, make sure your tone is welcoming and not accusatory. Do not treat people as if they are already guilty of mistreating your property, and do not feel like you need to explain yourself. For example, "please take your shoes off when indoors," is sufficient – no need to write, "Because I do not like germs, please take your shoes off the minute you walk inside."

Then, find out what your priorities are (things like smoking and pets are very important to be clear about), but also think about what is likely to happen: for example, if you have nice carpet in your bedroom and you want to specify that guests cannot eat in there, you might consider how likely it is for people to really eat in a bedroom, especially if there is another eating area available. One suggestion is to start out with fewer rules and then see what happens. If it turns out you need to make a rule about overnight guests because you live in a party town and people are going to clubs and bringing home strangers late at night, then you can add that in. Remember, you can alter the guest book at any time.

This is another case in which it is great to look at other people's rule book, which you can do by staying in Airbnb's.

Chapter Summary

A rulebook is a key part of the hosting experience. You must strike a delicate balance between getting your needs met and protecting your-self – while not coming off as a hostile or unwelcoming host. Ask your-self some key questions, think about who your guests are likely to be, check out your priorities, write a draft, and ask a good friend to look it over for you. Remember you can always edit it if it turns out that you missed something important.

Next Practical Actions to Take

- o Answer the list of questions provided
- o Draft your rulebook
- o Get a friend (preferably someone experienced as a host or at least as a guest) to look it over
- o Check out the rulebooks of other hosts
- o Post it to your page and tweak as necessary

CONCLUSION

We wish you the best of luck getting started on your journey to making significant money by hosting on Airbnb, whether or not you own property. A few things to remember as you go:

- Airbnb is all about the experience, so get into the spirit as you design your listing. It will earn you money in the long run

- Have a business mindset. It costs money to make money, but if you are smart and dedicated, and follow our advice, you will be able to start turning a profit, and then scaling it up until you might be able to leave your main job.

- Consider your possible online tools carefully. Lots of sites offer free and subscription-based services. Check for reviews before committing.

- Try dipping your toe in the water first by renting a room or a small property.

- Study your demographics and target the listing and the décor for them.

- Don't forget to get your gadgets

- Invest in photography. It is the most important thing that influences guests, along with great reviews – but the photography can happen immediately, the reviews take time.

- Try marketing your Airbnb using free channels like social media

- When in doubt, ask a professional – call an insurance agent, get an accountant to help with taxes, etc. – it'll save time and headaches later.

- Try hosting forums to get insider advice

- Start traveling on Airbnb so you know what you like and don't like.

- Have fun!

Next Practical Actions to Take

o   Are you ready to take the plunge? Look back through your notes and see what your remaining questions and concerns are. What areas do you need to research before making your decision more thoroughly?

www.ingramcontent.com/pod-product-compliance
Lightning Source LLC
Chambersburg PA
CBHW071713210326
41597CB00017B/2467

9781951698003